Career
Counselling

Counselling in Practice

Series editor: Windy Dryden
Associate editor: E. Thomas Dowd

Counselling in Practice is a series of books developed especially for counsellors and students of counselling, which provides practical, accessible guidelines for dealing with clients with specific, but very common, problems. Books in this series have become recognised as classic texts in their field, and include:

Career Counselling

SECOND EDITION

Robert Nathan and Linda Hill

SAGE Publications
London • Thousand Oaks • New Delhi

Dedication from the first edition

To my parents, who gave me such
a good start in life

LH

To my daughters Louise and Deborah,
who will always be special to me whatever
careers they choose

RN

© Robert Nathan and Linda Hill 2006

First edition published 1992
Reprinted 1994, 1996, 2000, 2002
This second edition first published 2006

SAGE Publications Ltd
1 Oliver's Yard
55 City Road
London EC1Y 1SP

SAGE Publications Inc.
2455 Teller Road
Thousand Oaks, California 91320

SAGE Publications India Pvt Ltd
B-42, Panchsheel Enclave
Post Box 4109
New Delhi 110 017

British Library Cataloguing in Publication data

A catalogue record for this book is available
from the British Library

ISBN 1–4129–0837–X (hbk)
ISBN 1–4129–0838–7 (pbk)

Library of Congress Control Number: 2005926976

Typeset by C&M Digitals (P) Ltd., Chennai, India
Printed on paper from sustainable resources
Printed and bound in Great Britain by Athenaeum Press, Gateshead

Contents

Foreword to the Second Edition

What is understood by the term 'career counselling' at the beginning of the 21st century? The more fluid and unpredictable nature of work seen today has been accompanied by an upsurge in demand to balance the differing parts of our lives. The need for financial and emotional security has not gone away. Many people still aspire to continuity of employment, and some still see progress in terms of promotion up a hierarchy, in spite of many years of downsizing, restructuring and 'delayering'. The chances are that clients coming for career counselling will have experienced several versions of 'reality' – from security of employment to the shock of redundancy, accelerated promotion or development, the pressure for profitability with fewer resources, and being faced with a complete turnaround of corporate values. Such a variety of experiences requires some key survival skills, including the ability to forge and maintain good relationships, the commitment to, and skill of, setting goals and the flexibility to respond to change.

When the amount of employer-led change is seen to be inequitable by employees, many have responded by demanding, through the annual employee survey, better career development opportunities in return for the 'self-managed career development' expected of them. In the competitive market place much is made of the McKinsey-coined term 'war on talent', as employers see the provision of career help as one way to support their goals of increasing retention of valued staff and becoming the 'employer of choice', as well as minimising any damage to their reputation by employees who leave.

These changes have been accompanied by an increasing demand for career support at key 'career transition' points, both by employers for their employees as well as by individuals acting on their own behalf. Thus, from the line manager and human resource professional, through to all those providing adult guidance, and the independent career counsellor, more and more people who are seen as prospective 'helpers' are being asked career-related questions.

These people are not solely career counsellors; they are making use of *career counselling skills*, along with many other skills and responsibilities. The chart in Chapter 1 (see p. 4) indicates the wide variety of contexts in which career help is sought, and this is increasingly the case within employing organisations. Hence this second edition of *Career Counselling* devotes an entire chapter to the place of career counselling within organisations.

The past 12 years have seen both a mushrooming of people with no allegiance to a professional code of conduct offering career-related help as well as a parallel desire to develop clear ethical and professional standards. Organisations as different as the British Association for Counselling and Psychotherapy

(BACP), the International Coaching Federation, the Chartered Institute of Personnel and Development (CIPD) Forum on Counselling and Career Management, and the Institute of Adult Guidance have all produced codes of ethics. Interest in professional career counselling training has also increased. Postgraduate qualifications in Career Counselling, such as the MSc offered by Birkbeck College, University of London, are seen as routes to a potential second career (see Appendix E).

Inevitably, people offering career help are being asked to assist with a wide variety of career-*related* issues (see the definition of career counselling on p. 2) in addition to the more traditional questions raised in career counselling (see Chapter 1). Many of the following examples draw on the survival skills mentioned in the first paragraph above:

Forging and maintaining good relationships

- How to network?
- How to 'partner'?
- How to manage 'upwards'?

The commitment and skill of setting goals

- Learning and development – what is on offer and what do I want?
- How can my learning goals fit in to my career goals?
- What kind of work–life balance do I want?

The flexibility to respond to change/managing uncertainty

- How to manage change effectively?
- How to transfer skills?
- How to manage flexible working patterns?
- How to acquire or re-learn skills?
- How to 'self-manage' in lean periods of employment?
- How to make the best use of time?
- How to deal with the stress caused by change and uncertainty?
- How to manage loss?

Self-employment and creativity

- Entrepreneurship – what it is and how to develop it?
- How to express creativity?
- How to make the choice of whether to make the leap?

These 'questions' are not only the province of the career counsellor. Some can be addressed effectively by many others, including guidance workers, coaches or mentors. In recent years, the question of how counselling, career counselling, coaching and mentoring differ or overlap is one we have heard regularly. The potential for confusion in both practitioners and clients underlines the importance of establishing clear boundaries. Practitioners need to know when they are offering career counselling, how to manage client expectations and contract accordingly with their clients. They need to be aware when they are operating outside of their skill set and be prepared to refer appropriately (Nathan, 2003).

Thus, the contexts in which career counselling takes place have multiplied, as much as people offering, and being approached for, career counselling have done so. In spite of, or perhaps because of, the vagaries of the employment marketplace, many clients who approach a career counsellor are still looking for 'the answer'. In our experience, no matter what the formally agreed contract has stipulated, that desire still remains covertly waiting in the wings. It needs to be acknowledged, but managed carefully.

Rob Nathan
London, January 2005

Acknowledgements

Career Counselling would never have been written were it not for the experience, support and skill of Linda Hill. Tragically, Linda died less than two years after the first edition was published. Not only did I lose a friend and colleague, but the profession of career counselling lost someone who brought a unique combination of warmth, wisdom and practicality. She knew how to get through to people in a way that always moved them forward.

For the second edition, I would like to thank Sue Moseley for her meticulous research; Eric Decker, Anton Fishman, Gilly Freedman and Antoinette Gaskell for their incisive comments on the new chapter Career Counselling in Organisations and other amended sections; and Jacey Graham, whose experience as a Diversity Consultant was invaluable in bringing that section up-to-date.

1 Introduction

People think I'm successful. I'm well paid, have a nice house and I'm good at my job. But I feel more and more dissatisfied with what I do.

I can't take a year off. How will it look on my CV? Employers will think I've been wasting my time.

Everyone's telling me I've got a lot of potential; but I've lost interest in studying.

When I married Sam, I thought he would be such a good provider. Now he's been made redundant.

The key words in these statements – successful, wasting, potential, provider, redundant – reflect a valuing of success and achievement. It is hardly surprising, therefore, that many people who approach a career counsellor, influenced by this pressure to succeed, may feel to some degree a failure in the eyes of partners, peers, employers or parents.

These assumptions, influences and values raise a number of considerations for career counsellors. Clients may want to turn their feelings of failure into a successful solution fairly urgently – to put things *right,* to find the *right* career, to feel all *right.* Their need to get things right may be transferred into expectations of the career counselling process to come up with the right answer, and to focus on extrinsic aspects of job satisfaction, such as money, status and working conditions, rather than considering their personal strengths and weaknesses.

Additional external pressures, such as keeping up the mortgage payments, saving face with friends or getting into the best college course tend to discourage clients from addressing any personal, and perhaps painful, emotional issues. These include understanding, accepting and building on changes in personal values, and coping with any negative feelings such as the loss and anger so often felt after losing a job.

What is career counselling?

Many people, if asked to define career counselling, would probably opt for something resembling the approach proposed by Parsons, as long ago as 1909. He wrote:

In the wise choice of vocation, there are three factors.

1 A clear understanding of yourself
2 A knowledge of the requirements and prospects in different lines of work
3 True reasoning on the relations of these two groups of facts.

This approach is based on the measurement, through testing, of the client's aptitudes and interests, followed by a recommendation by an 'expert' on occupations which provide a match in terms of the aptitudes and interests required. This process of 'talent matching' (sometimes known as the 'test and tell' approach) was the predominant form of assistance available to people seeking career help until the 1960s. For a number of reasons, we believe that career counsellors should not accept their clients' demands and expectations for 'advice on the best career'.

Firstly, making appropriate occupational decisions calls for the assistance of skilled and sensitive counselling: to reach the point where a rational decision can be made, emotional issues such as managing relationships, coping with loss and change and recovering from damaged self-esteem may first have to be addressed.

Secondly, since a 'job for life' is no longer a reality, lifelong decision-making skills are more conducive to the continuing challenge of making appropriate life and occupational choices, which are themselves increasingly interdependent.

Thirdly, employers require an increasingly flexible approach to their changing requirements, expecting employees to take responsibility for managing their own development, which might mean creating or accepting a 'development opportunity', such as a secondment, rather than waiting for promotion. There is also an increasing recognition that individuals themselves progress through a number of life stages (Super, 1980) and changes in their role requirements and responsibilities (Herriot, 1992).

Fourthly, making decisions is very much a matter of personal responsibility. A counselling approach empowers people to take such responsibility where they, not the counsellor, are the 'expert'.

The career counsellor, like all other counsellors, provides time, support, attention, skill and a structure which enables clients to become more aware of their own resources in order to lead a more satisfying life. We see career counselling as a *process which enables people to recognise and utilise their resources to make career-related decisions and manage career-related issues.* Although focusing on the work-related part of a person's life, it also takes into account the interdependence of career and non-career considerations.

This book focuses on the practice of career counselling. Figure 1.1 illustrates the overlap of career counselling with personal counselling, careers guidance and coaching. The larger 'Career counselling' circle indicates that the focus needs to remain on the *career* aspects of the client's life and the approach is primarily one rooted in *counselling*.

'Coaching' means different things to different people. People coming for career counselling are often unclear about their career direction. Coaching aims to enable people to become more effective in their current careers. There is overlap, but there is also a distinction.

In 1991 Hawthorn described 'guidance' as 'help for individuals to make choices about education, training and employment'. Today, the terms 'advice' and 'information', as well as 'guidance', are as commonly used to describe what careers services offer to potential users. We see this as a positive sign, being a move away from the directive and prescriptive connotations of the term 'guidance'. The *activities* of those involved in providing information, advice and guidance will involve counselling, as well as coaching, teaching, assessment and advocacy.

Figure 1.1   How career counselling overlaps with other forms of help

In addressing personal concerns regarding redundancy, retraining, relocation, retirement, relationships at work, promotion, career breaks and stress, career counselling necessarily overlaps with personal counselling.

The provision of career counselling in the UK

Unfortunately, in England the provision for adults seeking career help is very fragmented and largely uncoordinated. There is provision over much of the country, but it is not easy for anyone needing help to know what is on offer and who it is available for. It is unlikely that trained career counsellors staff the services. The Learning and Skills Council (LSC) is the national funding body for adult information, advice and guidance (IAG) throughout England. Local services vary from area to area, as services are delivered via IAG partnerships in each local region. IAG partnerships can include, for example, higher and further education careers services, voluntary bodies, private-sector providers and unions. There is no standard answer to how much services cost, or indeed whether they are free. Eligibility, too, varies, as some services are open to anyone, whilst others cater for those up to a certain level of qualification.

The national initiative 'Jobcentre Plus' is being created to integrate job centres, which give job advice, with benefits provision, by 2006. 'Learndirect' offers advice and information on education and training courses and is available to all nationally via the world wide web and telephone. 'Learndirect-futures' has online tools for career choice, as well as access to advisers. 'Waytolearn.co.uk' has been developed by the DfES to bring together information for people who want to learn (see Appendix C).

Help for young people in making career decisions is offered by careers teachers in schools and professionally qualified staff employed by the local Connexions partnership or careers service. In England, the 'cut off' age between services for

Figure 1.2 Who provides career help?

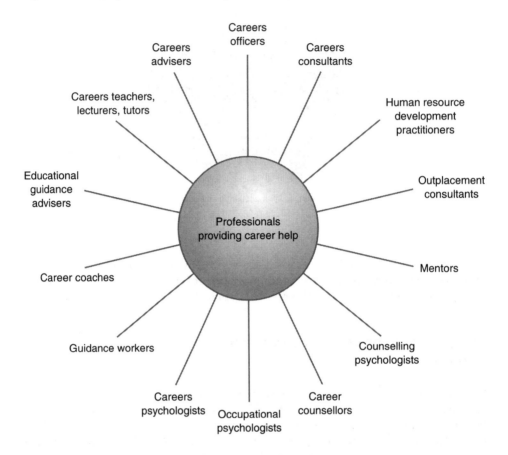

young people and adults is 19, whereas in Scotland, for example, an integrated service is available to people of all ages.

The various professionals involved in helping others to face career dilemmas are shown in Figure 1.2. All UK public universities provide a free careers service for their current students. Some also provide services to students once they have left, for which fees are usually charged. The University of London has a fee-charging careers service – C2 – available to *any* graduate, and at any stage of their career. For a more detailed study on careers services for employed people, see NICEC (2001).

The Department for Work and Pensions has 'Programme Centres' which offer the 'New Deal', a programme providing job search sessions, access to the internet and CV support, usually for a 13-week programme. Access is normally restricted to those unemployed for at least six months. Some services, known as 'Gateways', are available for people unemployed for less than six months.

An increasing number of employers offer career help to their staff, for example:

- career development discussions to clarify career direction and/or development plans;
- workshops for 'high potential' people to assess and reflect on their suitability for general management or partnership;
- career support for specific groups, such as graduates, women or ethnic minorities;
- career management 'centres' or 'clinics', available for all on a confidential basis;
- learning and development advice, information and counselling, to support career development;
- outplacement help with job hunting for people whose jobs are being made redundant;
- career counselling for 'redeployees' at a time of restructuring;
- pre-retirement planning services;
- advice, information and self-assessment exercises via an Intranet site; and
- coaching and mentoring.

See Chapter 7, *Career Counselling in Organisations,* for a more detailed look at this area. See also the NICEC report (2004) on managing careers in large organisations.

Some national organisations, for example, the Armed Forces, the Law Society, the Royal Institute of Chartered Surveyors, the Institute of Public Relations and the Royal National Institute for the Deaf, also offer career help to special groups.

Because government-backed career counselling provision for adults in the UK continues to be so fragmented, there has been a mushrooming of independent services, staffed by specialist career counsellors, occupational psychologists and counselling psychologists. These services differ in their use of psychometric tests. There are some services which still offer a 'test and tell' approach, in which the client is given a series (or 'battery') of tests measuring aptitudes, occupational interests and aspects of personality, the results of which are then interpreted by a consultant psychologist and a report with recommendations subsequently written. Other career counsellors may make little or no use of tests, but use counselling skills to assist clients to make sense of occupational and other aspects of their lives. The connection between work and non-work life has increasingly become the focus of anyone helping adults with career dilemmas, whether it be the burnt-out executive who wants to spend more time with the family or the single mum trying to make ends meet.

Outplacement consultants offer specific help to executives and others facing a job loss. This may involve some counselling to assist recovery from the trauma of the redundancy, but more usually focuses on coaching and support in job hunting. Such services are often paid for by the company as part of a severance package. Outplacement companies are now broadening their services to include career reviews and career-planning workshops, although the traditional job search activities remain the core of what they offer. They are also increasing the provision of services via the Internet, and setting up advisory centres 'in-house' for staff below executive level.

Confusingly, some practitioners who describe themselves as career counsellors are not doing career counselling in the sense that they subscribe to a counselling philosophy or have training in counselling skills.

Although traditionally offered on a one-to-one basis, career counselling is increasingly being offered in groups. There are a number of advantages of working in groups:

- they are economical to run;
- a group provides a wider range of resources, ideas and information;
- participants realise that they are not alone, as others are facing similar issues;
- mutual support is readily available both during and after the group's existence;
- there is less dependency on the career counsellor as 'expert'; and
- groups provide more opportunities to use active techniques such as coaching in job-hunting skills.

Many such groups are run within employing organisations, and may be focused primarily on occupational issues, more broadly on life and career development, or may form part of a positive action programme, for example, directed at supporting minority groups. Some independent agencies offer 'open' career and life-review workshops, whilst there is government backing for projects to assist the long-term unemployed to assess their job-related skills and receive support and coaching in job hunting. A combination of group and individual approaches may be used as part of a career counselling programme. For example, the administration of psychometric tests can be done in a group, followed by individual feedback and counselling, followed by interview practice in a group. Most of the approaches and techniques described in this book are amenable to either a one-to-one or group approach.

What characterises an effective career discussion was an issue addressed through research conducted by Hirsch et al. (2001). They highlighted how important the approach of clients receiving career counselling is to the success of it: they should 'try to be as objective and realistic as possible, being open to feedback …'.

Box 1.1 summarises the services which professional career counsellors may offer.

Box 1.1 The services which may be offered by career counsellors

One-to-one career counselling:

- one-off consultation;
- a series of one-to-one meetings without assessment;
- a series of one-to-one meetings with questionnaire and test administration, feedback and counselling;
- a series of career counselling meetings with written assignments (but no tests); and
- a series of career counselling meetings with tests and written assignments.

Group career counselling:

- career development workshops (also known by other titles, such as career planning, review workshops or self-development groups).

Access to careers, learning and development information via a library or the Internet.

Coaching in job-hunting techniques, including CV writing and interview practice: this may be one to one or group based.

The majority of career counsellors provide their clients with access to careers information in some form. An approach to providing occupational information which is consistent with a counselling ethos is examined in detail in Chapter 5. Some career counsellors make use of web-based occupational information and other careers guidance tools. This is a specialised topic for which there is no space in this book, although Appendices C and D refer to useful resources. Job-hunting techniques are not the domain of this book, but are detailed in Floyed and Nathan (2002).

Who should read this book?

This book will assist anyone offering career support, from specialist career counsellors and advisers to line managers. The skills and techniques will also be of value to other practitioners who encounter people who need help in choosing, changing or developing their careers. Practising counsellors and psychotherapists, whether they are working with individuals or groups, will find the structured approach and the specific occupational considerations of benefit when a job-related concern is affecting a client's well-being. Other professionals who use career counselling skills and techniques, or who offer career counselling within another role, will find the book a thorough and practical guide to the process of career counselling and the different techniques available. This group includes human resources and training managers, recruitment and outplacement consultants, careers officers and learning and development advisers, who may need to assist staff and clients in addressing career-related issues as part of their role. For the sake of simplicity and clarity, throughout the book we refer to 'career counsellors' to cover all categories.

Although the main focus is on work with adults, the book will also be valuable to anyone helping young people to make occupational decisions. Abbey and Graham (1996) focus more specifically on careers work with young people. This book is a manual, not an exposition of theory. A detailed consideration of career choice and development theories will be found in Arthur et al. (1989).

Our approach to career counselling

This book is based on our own experience of providing and teaching career counselling. We draw on the work of several counselling theorists, including the client-centred approach of Carl Rogers (1965), the staged approach of Gerard Egan (2002), and some solution-focused techniques (for example, O'Connell, 1998). Krumboltz (1976) described some behavioural approaches which challenge, for example, a client's 'self-limiting beliefs'. Our approach is also influenced by some of the key career theorists, including Holland (1983), Super (1980) and, more recently, the work of Cochran (1997). For readers interested in psychodynamic approaches in career counselling, see Jacinto et al. (2000). This book does not describe the particular theories in detail, but will refer to them at different points in the text to illustrate how they relate to practice.

Taylor (1985) identified a number of critical questions applicable to the practice of career counselling:

To what extent should the client's feelings be expressed and dealt with, or is the focus on the rational aspects of decision making? It is unrealistic to expect that all clients will be ready to consider rationally the choices available. Career counselling should allow clients' feelings to be expressed where such expression will further the goals of career counselling.

For some people, the degree of anxiety felt about a work or non-work problem will need to be addressed either prior to or concurrent with career counselling. For example, a divorcee may need to address feelings of loss while seeking to support herself financially.

For other people, various 'self-limiting beliefs' may be contributing to unproductive behaviour not only in making rational decisions about a career, but also at work (see Chapter 4).

Who should collect or provide the information – client, counsellor or both? We believe that this is a joint responsibility. The two main types of information the client needs in order to make an occupational decision are personal information and information about the nature of different jobs and work environments.

Our practice is to make use of various sources of information about a client, including self-assessment exercises, psychometric tests, and information emerging from discussion in counselling sessions. Both the counsellor and the client are information collectors, although the collection belongs to the client.

Our contract is that the client is responsible for researching information about jobs and work environments, whilst the counsellor points the client towards sources (see Chapter 5).

Who is the expert (that is, who should be in charge, deciding how the issues raised should be handled) – client, counsellor or both? We believe that clients are very much the experts as far as handling their own problems is concerned. It can be easy for clients to give up their power to the career counsellor and adopt a passive approach to the 'expert advice giver'. We like to involve clients in choosing whether to take tests. We also encourage clients to listen as active participants to and reflect upon tape recordings of feedback discussions and researching options. Whilst some counsellors and clients may have misgivings about the tape recording of sessions, we have found this to be a powerful and effective tool (see Chapter 5).

Who should have the responsibility for making the decision – client or counsellor? What we are describing in this book is an approach to career counselling firmly rooted in a counselling, not a didactic or advisory, ethos. The responsibility for decision making is therefore with the client, whilst the counsellor is responsible for facilitating the process.

What should the predominant counsellor style be – directive, collaborative, interpretive or reflective? Career counsellors need to be able to adapt their styles according to the needs of the client and the stage of the career counselling process (see Box 1.2). A prescriptive style is inappropriate to the approach described in this book. A reflective style may well be appropriate early in the career counselling, but may also be appropriate together with tentative interpretations and a more challenging style later on. In the final stages of career counselling, when action is probably being addressed, a coaching style may be appropriate.

Box 1.2 Stages of Career Counselling

Stage	Client tasks	Counsellor tasks
Screening, contracting, exploring	Making a preliminary assessment of the suitability of career counselling. Undertaking written preparation. Testing out readiness for and appropriateness of career counselling. Openness to exploring presenting concerns and influences on career and educational development and choices. Clarifying expectations of career counselling. Discussing and agreeing contract.	Educating and informing clients about career counselling, through written, spoken and face-to-face communication. Evaluating the client's readiness for and appropriateness of career counselling, suggesting more suitable forms of help, if necessary. Building rapport, facilitating exploration. Establishing contract (i.e. confidentiality, structure etc.).
Enabling client's understanding	Considering the questions: Who am I? Where am I now? What do I want? Where do I want to be? Completing self-assessment exercises, psychometric tests and questionnaires, as appropriate. Being prepared to tackle the question 'What's stopping me?' Researching information on work opportunities.	Facilitating exploration of feelings and beliefs associated with career concern/issues. Helping client to identify important themes and integrate self-understanding. Making appropriate use of self-assessment exercises and psychometric tests and questionnaires. Helping client to overcome blocks to action, using challenging skills, if appropriate. Signposting information on work possibilities.
Action, outcome and endings	Completing decision-making and action-planning exercises. Developing options and choosing between options. Putting decision into action. Agreeing research tasks, if appropriate. Addressing fears of change. Evaluating need for continued support. Reviewing progress made towards objectives during career counselling.	Enabling clients to generate ideas and choose between them. Supporting client in developing and monitoring action plan. Agreeing research tasks, if appropriate. Helping clients face ambivalence about the future. Exploring client's need for continued support. Stressing importance of maintaining momentum. Helping client to identify resources and sources of support.

The solution-focused approach can be very effective in career counselling. Being *solution-* rather than *problem*-focused, it can be especially relevant when the client in career counselling is ready to *do* something, but needs help in describing, and committing to, the small steps required to get going (see Chapter 4).

The entire career counselling process can facilitate clients' in managing their careers more effectively. Since some clients who come for individual career counselling undervalue their strengths and skills, a supportive style can affirm their intrinsic value. When it is appropriate, a cathartic style may enable clients to free themselves from negative emotions through, for example, crying and expressing anger. See Heron (1990) for a fuller discussion on styles of intervention.

What should be discussed in career counselling? The client's personal/emotional problems, self-appraisal, decision making, test results, information on options, evaluating options, job hunting? Career counselling recognises the interdependence of problems and that personal issues need to be addressed within the career counselling process. The question of when personal counselling is more appropriate than career counselling is addressed in Chapter 7. Similarly, a career counsellor will need to use a coaching approach when addressing job-hunting issues, or refer appropriately (see Figure 1.1).

Summary of the contents

Chapter 2 examines the kinds of issues and dilemmas that clients commonly bring to career counselling. These include issues associated with particular life stages and events; the balance between work and non-work aspects of life; challenges in making or implementing career decisions; disruption brought about by change in organisations; and performance-related issues. In each case we discuss the different kinds of concerns presented, any underlying issues and the implications for career counsellors.

The next four chapters are concerned with the stages in the career counselling process, which are summarised in Box 1.2, together with suggested 'tasks' and responsibilities for both the career counsellor and the client.

If clients are thoroughly briefed about the nature of the service, and can decide for themselves whether career counselling is appropriate, they are more likely to gain from the career counselling than if they had arrived with little or no preparation. Chapter 3 addresses the important but often underemphasised screening and contracting stages, during which the client can become clear about what to expect from career counselling, and the counsellor can explore the likelihood of being able to help this person meet his or her expectations. An initial meeting can be used as a preliminary discussion, without full commitment on either side, and can fulfil a number of purposes:

- it allows clients to 'opt out' without further commitment;
- it enables career counsellors to evaluate the readiness of clients for career counselling;

- it educates clients about the career counselling process, beyond any written documentation; and
- it allows both counsellor and client to discuss the most appropriate 'contract', including the usefulness of assessment tests for this person.

The development of self-understanding is central to Chapters 4 and 5. Chapter 4 looks at the process of enabling clients to address the questions 'Who am I?', 'What do I want?' and 'What is stopping me?' For some clients, greater self-understanding is all that is needed, and this may promote new energy or a change of attitude. For others, self-understanding is just the first stage. They want career counselling to help them make decisions or formulate action plans. Chapter 4 also addresses the crucial stage between promoting self-understanding and taking action – that of enabling clients to reduce the effects of any blocks to action. In particular, we look at the importance of assisting clients to evaluate the impact of self-limiting beliefs and values. The chapter presents many in-session approaches, as well as between-session home assignments, and shows how these can be woven into career counselling.

Chapter 5 describes how psychometric tests and questionnaires can aid the career counselling process. Tests can be appropriate and beneficial if they are administered sensitively and at the right point in the career counselling. If tests are used together with other tools, such as interest questionnaires and self-assessment exercises, they contribute towards, but do not dominate, any feedback discussions. All 'data' produced during the career counselling process can be of value. Data may include written preparation by clients, feedback by the counsellor and responses by clients to such feedback. Chapter 5 also looks at the role of occupational, and other, information in career counselling, and the kinds of information that career counsellors need to know.

Many counselling practitioners find it hard to enable their clients to move on from the exploration and clarification stages of the career counselling process to the 'decision-making' and 'action' stages when these are appropriate. In Chapter 6, practical techniques of encouraging clients to make and follow through their decisions are described. These include exercises for choosing between options, completing action plans and addressing fears of change. Chapter 6 also considers the value of 'follow-up', an aspect of career counselling which is often overlooked.

Chapter 7 looks at the reasons why career counselling is increasingly made available by employers, and the kind of areas that are addressed in such 'career conversations'. A key section of this chapter considers the dilemmas facing career counsellors working within an organisational context. These include 'Who is the client?', aspects of confidentiality and the question of the use, and potential misuse, of power in the career counselling relationship.

The boundary between career and personal counselling, the question of referral, and working with 'third parties' such as employers or partners, are some of the key issues for career counsellors which are explored in Chapter 8. Career counsellors need general counselling skills. These are summarised in this chapter, together with a description of some of the areas of specialist knowledge useful for career counsellors, for example, an understanding of factors relevant in career management.

Like all counsellors, career counsellors must maintain good professional practice in order to maximise the quality of the service provided, the protection of clients and their own well-being. The elements of monitoring and evaluation, non-managerial supervision and counsellor self-management are described in Chapter 9.

The book is illustrated throughout with case-study examples which are derived from individuals who have presented their concerns to a career counsellor. Names and identifying material have been changed to safeguard client confidentiality. Many of the practical exercises illustrated throughout the text can be found in Appendix H, for ease of use.

2 Issues Brought to Career Counselling

Individuals approach career counselling when they, or perhaps someone else, have identified issues in their lives which they perceive to be primarily *career* related, and therefore appropriate for discussion with someone offering a *career* counselling service. This might be a service offered by an employer or an independent service. However, we believe it naive and unrealistic to help clients solve their *career* problems without allowing them to see the wider ramifications of their situation. In order to find the best solution to a career-related issue, we often find that clients need to examine their career problem in the context of their lives as a whole. This may be necessary for the following reasons:

- The desire for a more interesting job may be a reflection of a life stage or event outside of work.
- Problems can be linked (for example, a relationship difficulty at home may have precipitated a crisis at work).
- A long-time problem which has been tolerated may have become intolerable (for example, continuing relationship difficulties at work may have been tolerated until a 'last straw' incident).
- Lack of career advancement may be partly linked to poor interpersonal skills.
- Anger towards 'company policy' may reflect a general dislike, for example, of being controlled.
- An apparently realistic constraint (for example, a recession) may belie the need to focus on the emotions engendered by personal difficulties.
- Dissatisfaction with job content or career attainment may conceal a deeper lack of self-esteem.
- A client presenting as highly stressed may have chosen a job for its potential monetary rewards, but many years of being in unsatisfying work have taken their toll.

This chapter will discuss the kinds of clients who come for career counselling, the concerns they typically bring, the problems which may sometimes underlie the presenting issues, and the implications for the practice of career counselling.

Firstly, we discuss issues which may be typical of a certain stage or time of life, for example, the 'mid-life crisis'. We then examine work–life balance issues, inability to make a career decision, difficulty in implementing a choice, problems arising from change at work (including redundancy), performance issues, relationship problems, and issues connected with creativity. These categories are not, of course, mutually exclusive and many clients will need help with problems in several categories.

Stress management and career counselling

Much of this chapter addresses issues that, by implication, challenge clients' abilities to manage the 'work' part of their lives effectively. Whilst this is not a book on stress management, career counsellors will see many clients who are experiencing difficulty in coping. Thus, some knowledge of the nature of stress, its causes and strategies for coping with it will be useful (see, for example, Allen, 2002).

Today there is greater pressure than ever before for employees to perform well, and to do so with fewer resources. Job security can never be taken for granted, and the inevitability of change is an ever-present concern.

It is helpful for career counsellors to identify whether an apparently stress-induced problem is, in fact, related to any of the issues described below, and thus amenable to a career counselling approach. Making a choice of job and lifestyle based on clear information about strengths (and weaknesses), interests and values, together with a consideration of external resources (such as support and commitments) may contribute to 'stress management'; but job and lifestyle choice will not be the only factors to consider. For more generic help with stress management, a solution-focused approach could be beneficial (see O'Connell, 1998).

An individual or shared problem?

Clients coming for career counselling may be helped initially by receiving literature detailing some of the more common problems experienced. This in itself can reduce a sense of isolation ('I'm not the only one') and allow an early airing of the problem. Box 2.1 shows some of the common questions asked of career counsellors.

Box 2.1 Common questions which clients bring to career counselling

- I feel at a crossroads in my career. Can you help me decide which way to go?
- I am shortly to be made redundant. Can you help me plan my future?
- I think I know what I want, but I can't seem to motivate myself. Can you help me explore what might be holding me back?
- I haven't worked for several years. Can you help me assess my true strengths and build up my confidence?
- I have growing feelings of dissatisfaction with my career. Can you help me reflect on the suitability of the career I have chosen?
- I'm not happy in my current job, but I am not sure whether I should change careers or just need a change of employer. Can you help me decide?
- Nothing seems to interest or excite me. I'm at a loss. Can you help me identify what really motivates me?
- I'm interested in so many things. Can you help me focus?
- My work and home life are out of balance. Can you help me gain some perspective and, consequently, a more satisfying balance?
- I think I know what I want, but I'm not being offered any openings. I'm uncertain whether I am aiming too high or if I need help improving my self-presentation. Can you help me address what could move me forward?

Every client coming for career counselling brings a unique response to whatever problems he or she is facing. A fundamental principle of any counselling intervention is that clients are allowed to find their own unique solution to a problem, *even if the problem being faced is a common one.*

Career counsellors must recognise that an individual's needs, aspirations and career opportunities are affected by factors like gender, class, race, disability and age. For example, although there are some general principles to be borne in mind in counselling a client who has been made redundant, it is important for a career counsellor working with a black woman who has been made redundant to be sensitive to how her feelings and experiences as a woman and as a black person affect her situation.

Thomas (1990) suggests the following questions for counsellors:

1   What is the ostensible problem that brings the client to counselling, and how common is this problem within the client's age group, gender group and cultural group?
2   Among people of this client's age, gender and cultural type, what other problems and conditions are often linked to, or underlie, the client's apparent problem?
3   Which attitudes held by society towards people of the client's age, gender and cultural type influence such a client's problem? Furthermore, how free is the client to choose what ambitions, lifestyles and methods of personal/social adjustment he or she will adopt?
4   How can the level of physical, cognitive, emotional and social development of clients at this life stage, of this gender and of this cultural type help determine the counselling techniques that are likely to be most suitable?

However, Thomas suggests that career counsellors should be wary of trying to fit their clients into 'normal' groups and risk losing sight of that particular person's individuality – it is that individuality which provides clients with the energy needed to make decisions and manage their problems:

While descriptive group data can suggest questions to pose and areas of counselees' lives to investigate, the success of treating any case depends ultimately on how artfully the counselor discovers – by means of interviews, observations, tests and intuition – how the variables in each client's life are woven together to form that person's special pattern of individuality. (Thomas, 1990)

Clients often come to career counselling feeling that they 'ought' to be different in some way from how they actually are; their individuality has not been allowed to flourish. Some of these feelings stem from parental values which have been internalised, so that people try to conform to or live up to parental expectations. For example, a classical education at a boys' public school paid for by parents who want their son to enter a profession puts one set of pressures on a person, quite different from the pressures placed on a girl with a mother who has played a traditional homemaking role and whose schooling has channelled her into taking secretarial studies. Carl Rogers describes the imposition of 'conditions of worth' on a child by parents. He defines a fully functioning person as a person who is fully open to experience, with access to all the available data in a situation, and who is free to 'discover that course of action which would come closest to satisfying all his needs in that situation' (Rogers, 1965). Conditions of worth limit the natural development and unfolding of potential and personality, and stunt or slant a person's development in various ways. When people do not live according to parental expectations (whether through trying but failing, or through rebellion), feelings of failure and confusion can be engendered:

> Mary had gone to a very traditional girls' grammar school. Her father was a manual worker and her mother served in a cake shop. Although Mary did well at school and stayed on to study for A levels, she never thought she was clever enough to go to university. No one in her family had ever been, and Mary didn't bother applying. She left school with three good A-level passes during a recession and was unemployed for several months before finding a clerical job in a bank. She did well there, but found the work boring. At the age of 26, after some encouragement from her boyfriend, she decided to apply for a part-time degree course in law. Her father couldn't understand why she wanted to do the course, saying, 'You've got a good job already.' Mary was offered a place, and intended to begin that autumn. However, at the last minute she found she was quite unable to bring herself to go along to the course.

Through career counselling, Mary realised that her feelings about coming from what she described as a 'working-class background' were giving rise to ambivalence about doing the course. She remembered that when she had started at the grammar school, some of the girls had called her 'common', sneered at her accent and her clothing and joked about her mother working in the local cake shop. The parents of these girls were from the professional classes. At some level Mary felt that law degrees were only for middle-class people, and that she was 'not good enough'. She expressed a strong fear that she would be 'found out'. Her boyfriend seemed to be the catalyst for Mary to come for career counselling and, possibly for the first time in her life, address what *she* actually wanted.

Even if discrimination and oppression ended today, career counsellors would face a 'backlog' for many years to come of individuals from 'minority' groups who have experienced discrimination in education and employment, in addition to the negative effects of oppression which, like Mary, people have internalised. Some guidelines for career counsellors when working with clients who are from 'minority' groups are given in Chapter 8.

Within this framework, we will now consider the people who come for career counselling, and the common problems they bring.

Life-stage problems

Life stages, and their associated tasks, were identified as far back as 2,500 years ago, as quoted in *The Sayings of the Fathers* (The Talmud). Fourteen ages of man were indicated, each with its own developmental tasks. More recently, Shakespeare outlined seven ages of man in *As You Like It*. Since the 1970s, there has been a plethora of stage theories, the most influential including Levinson et al. (1978), Super (1957, 1980) and Sheehy (1976). Certain myths have probably developed about the kind of tasks, attitudes and behaviours *expected* of people in each stage. For example, men in their forties are supposed to go through the 'male menopause'. Such myths can act as an unhelpful pressure; if young adults under the age of 25 are supposed to have a high drive to succeed, or people in their late twenties are expected to be 'settling down', clients who find themselves with a low desire to achieve at 22 or a desire to travel at 29 may feel guilty for feeling different from what is expected of them, or they might think that something is wrong with them. In this section we look at six life stages and some of the associated career counselling issues.

School leavers

The concerns for school leavers revolve around 'what next?'. The relatively unknown world of work or further study awaits young people. They want knowledge and guidance, but they are also going through an important transition from the struc-tured lifestyle in school to the less structured world outside.

Many young people will be subject to influences from parents and peers, and will be trying to establish their own meaning and identity out of these, perhaps conflicting, influences. For example, Jonathan's parents had hoped that he would go on to university, but his friends were leaving school and going directly into jobs. Their purchasing power was substantial compared to his. Jonathan did quite poorly in his A levels, and came for career counselling at the behest of his parents.

From our experience of working with young people, it is important to establish a contract clearly and directly with the young person. Contracting is covered in more detail in Chapter 3. Additionally, the nature of the referral can tell the career counsellor something of the problem and the client's relationship to the problem. This is discussed further in Chapter 8.

The twenties

People in this age band are faced with the task of finally leaving the parental home and establishing their own individual identity. This time of life usually involves some 'trying out' of different jobs, and clients may bring to career counselling their 'first job blues'. Problems may have arisen owing to difficulties experienced in adjusting to the requirements of the job. Questions such as 'Is this really what work is about?' may be on the agenda. Disappointment with the values and ethos of the work environment may be combined with a sense of loss for the 'certainties' provided by school or university. There may be a reassessment of ideals about 'changing the world'. We also see the effects of educational decisions made at the age of 15 or 16 coming home to roost.

Confusion concerning the boundaries of their competence may surface: 'I did well in school, but I wasn't prepared for this.' Fitting in socially may also be a consideration.

Age 30 transition

This is a common stage for people to seek career counselling, as it is a time of questioning the values and decisions of the twenties. Careers and relationships are particularly liable to be reassessed. People may realise that they have drifted or been pushed into a career path. Now they want to take more control of their life and career direction. The consideration of settling down with a partner and family may be an issue, whether or not the person wants it, and the age 30 transition can be a particularly difficult time for women. Clients are often more prepared to reflect on their initial commitments than they might have been a few years earlier.

The thirties

Many of our clients in their thirties are 'waking up' to their own mortality. The expectation of this stage is that people will want to be more settled into a career, a relationship and a particular lifestyle. Those clients who are not conforming to this expectation, either by choice or otherwise, may bring an additional sense of failure to career counselling.

Clients who are conforming to this expectation may want help making solid plans for the future. Some may not be progressing in their chosen career as quickly as they would like, and seek assistance in understanding why this may be so. Others may be having difficulty in managing relationships at work, and want to review their personal strengths and weaknesses rather than just their suitability for certain careers. One choice may be to develop their careers into management or to stay in a more technical, specialised function. Another could be the consideration of suitability for self-employment.

Midlife transition

This can be a most confused time of life. It can bring a sense of physical decline. With increasing age, the length of retraining required, financial and personal commitments and the perceived difficulties of adjusting to a new lifestyle, a second or even third career can seem increasingly difficult to attain. In spite of outward signs of success, the person approaching the career counsellor may feel a sense of emptiness – a lack of fulfilment. There may be an acute recognition of the gap between early aspirations and actual achievements. There may be a concern to do something 'more worthwhile'. Career counsellors could be asked to help clients recover their 'spark'.

For some women, this may be a time when, after bringing up their children, they want to return to a full-time career. Career counsellors could be asked to give help with assessing capabilities, restoring confidence and, in particular, looking at transferable skills.

Colin (1979) discusses the symptoms and causes of the so-called 'mid-life crisis'. For many people it can be an opportunity for development, growth and fulfilment – see Clay (1989) for cases which demonstrate this.

Forty-five plus

The possibility or reality of redundancy can hit at any time. Its effects will depend on many factors, including previous experience of redundancy, expectation of re-employment, previous sense of self-worth, the existence of a career plan, support from a partner and others, financial resources and practical as well as financial help from the employer. It can hit people particularly hard in this stage of life.

Yet, with an ageing population, more employers are offering 'older-worker-friendly' employment policies (for example, B&Q and Asda). Although the prospect of retirement may begin to emerge for some, others are having to and, in some cases, wanting to work beyond the traditional retirement age.

Some people may want to consider developing new, or reviving old, interests. The stereotype of 'slowing down' may be a concern for someone who is wanting to begin a new career. The prospect of an abrupt shift to leisure may cause fear or apprehension in some people whereas, with increased life expectancies, the post-retirement period should perhaps be seen much more positively as a 'Third Age' in which people can continue to grow and develop (Schuller and Walker, 1990).

Some clients may want help in 'making sense of' or coming to terms with their past decisions so that they can more smoothly pass on to the next stage of their lives.

Implications for career counsellors

Life-stage theory can be useful to career counsellors in considering the possibility of age-related issues being relevant to clients, but it should not become a straitjacket for neatly pigeonholing a person, as the same kind of problems may arise at different life stages. Examples include disillusionment with a career choice or the questioning of previously held values. It is more appropriate to make a mental note of possible areas of concern to the client at this time in his or her life. No stage theory can interpret how an individual reacts to a particular situation.

Normal age-related problems are sometimes mistaken for signs of serious emotional disturbance. According to Moreland (1979), cycles of stability interspersed with crisis are natural to human development and should not be considered pathological. Information about life stages can come as a great relief to clients.

The consideration of how a person's values might be changing according to their life stage is an important one for career counsellors. Values may also change as a result of events or experiences in the individual's life. Box 2.2 summarises some situations which can cause an individual to rethink his or her values.

Box 2.2 Life events affecting values

- Bereavement
- Redundancy
- Divorce
- Long-term unemployment
- Injury or disease causing temporary or permanent disability
- Recovery from alcoholism or other addiction
- Recovery from mental illness
- Return home after long period of travel
- Returning to 'civilian life' after a period in uniformed service
- Birth of children
- Children leaving home

Problems to do with work–life balance

Work–life balance issues are of some concern to many clients coming for career counselling. For a few, they are crucial. Whilst the concern to address the lack of balance does often arise with people in their late twenties and beyond, many more younger people are setting out to avoid what they see as the trap into which their elders fell.

'Downsized' employers, increased levels of competition and lower profit margins are just a few of the factors that have contributed to pressures for higher levels of performance, and with fewer resources. This means longer hours and overwork for people who no doubt have large financial outgoings. Such people may feel they have no choice but to continue in the same employment, even when it no longer matches their interests and values. Many more women now want to combine paid employment with mothering, whilst others, notably single mothers, may have little choice when they are the sole source of income.

Thus a common question clients want to address is how their work fits into the rest of their lives. Issues about work–life balance often arise for clients who are going through life transitions, or who have, or are considering having, children:

> Laura had been working in a routine clerical job for ten years, since she left school; work had held very little significance for her. She was referred for career counselling by a bereavement counsellor, following the death of her husband. She now needed more satisfaction from her work.

> Tariq worked long, anti-social hours in the catering industry. With two small children, he was beginning to feel that he was missing out on family life, and wanted a job which would allow him a better balance between work and family.

> Althea had brought up two boys and a girl and had never worked outside the home. At the age of 36, she now wanted to get a job.

> Malcolm was a self-employed builder, married to a nurse. After they had their first child, Malcolm's wife said she would like to go back to work and develop her career. His work was suffering because of a recession, and he wanted to discuss the implications of becoming a 'house husband'.

> Jenny had been trained in teaching, but gave it up when she married. With two school-age children, she wanted to explore the possibilities of returning to work.

Consideration of the work–life balance may not initially be on the client's agenda in approaching a career counsellor, but it may need to be addressed if, for example, the expression of a client's creativity at work is blocked and there appears to be more opportunity to develop it outside work.

When a client has work–life balance issues, an underlying conflict of values often exists, as the following case study illustrates:

> Sandra came to career counselling saying that she was feeling 'burnt out' with social work, and tired and frustrated about all the reorganisations and cuts made to the services in her local authority. Although she was presenting with the career need to assess alternative possibilities for the future, during the first meeting it emerged that she had just discovered she was pregnant. At the age of 40, she had
>
> *(Continued)*

(Continued)

recently become very close to a man with whom she worked, and they had begun a sexual relationship. Having been a determinedly successful 'career woman' all her working life, she was feeling very agitated and confused about this relationship, her pregnancy and the implications for her future. Sandra was feeling torn in two directions. One side of her desperately wanted to move in with her friend and have a child 'before it's too late'. The other side of her felt that to do this would mean abandoning her many work responsibilities and 'causes' and sinking into a cosy and stereotyped domesticity which would be a betrayal of much of what she had fought against all her working life.

The kind of choices available to Jeanetta, however, seem very different:

My name is Jeanetta. I am 24 and I have two kids, four and six months. I have been on and off welfare since my kids were born. I started working in fast food when I was in high school. The work was OK but I was on my feet all day. It was hard to keep working while being pregnant. The baby's father didn't stay around long – we were fighting a lot anyway. When my oldest was three, I found a neighbour who would watch her and I got a job in telemarketing. I didn't like the work – and three months later, I got pregnant again. I didn't really want to, but now I love my youngest. I've been quite depressed, especially after my grandmother died last year. After I left the job, I found I didn't have the energy to get things done anymore. I'm now not sure what kind of work I can do – maybe work in an office. The kids are the most important part of my life – I just love watching them grow; when they hug and tell me they love me, I feel like nothing else matters. (Adapted from McDonald, 2002)

It is important to be aware that low-income single mothers such as Jeanetta are likely to suffer from sexual, class and racial discrimination (Corcoran et al., 1984), The lone responsibility for bringing up children, the possibility of domestic violence and the need to negotiate bureaucratic government systems can give rise to high levels of stress. Career counselling can still be of great help to Jeanetta, along with access to employment market information, coaching and rehearsal in job-hunting skills, and access to relevant support services. To combat her sense of isolation, Jeanetta might find it useful to join a job search support group.

For up-to-date discussions on work–life balance issues, see the online Work–Family Research Newsletter (www.bc.edu/bc__org/avp/wfnetwork/newsletter).

Implications for career counsellors

The career counsellor needs to encourage the client to make a decision about the balance between work and the rest of life which is appropriate for that individual at that time of his or her life. In order to be able to do this, career counsellors must be careful not to allow their own beliefs about male and female roles in relation to family and work to influence the career counselling. Clients who are in the process of making a significant change to the balance between work and the rest of their lives may require some support from the career counsellor over an extended period.

A knowledge of life stages and the issues which typically arise is useful when dealing with work–life balance issues, as is knowing about alternatives to full-time employment (see Chapter 7).

Discussion of work–life balance often uncovers unresolved personal issues, and the career counsellor should be sensitive to the potential need for referral for personal counselling.

An appreciation of the stresses facing low-income clients, together with knowledge of the available support services, is vital for anyone providing career help for this group.

Decision-making problems

'I can't decide what to do' is probably the most common presenting problem with which career counsellors are faced. It may simply be the case that a client lacks the occupational information on which to base a decision, but an inability to make a career decision is more likely to stem from other causes, as Derek's case study demonstrates:

> Derek was from Wales. He did exceptionally well at school, and went to Cambridge to read natural sciences. At first, although he felt out of place at times, he did very well. However, during his third year he became very unmotivated towards his studies, and this seemed to be connected with his lack of career direction. Exploration in several career counselling sessions revealed that Derek had never made a single educational decision himself, but had dutifully followed the advice of his teachers. In spite of his ability, he was also frightened of making a commitment to a particular career, in case it was the 'wrong' one and he failed.

Ford (2002) views self-esteem – the level of satisfaction with self – as central to the ability to make a career decision. Raising self-awareness through career counselling can contribute to building self-esteem.

Some clients present as not *knowing* who they are; we often hear the statement 'I don't know my strengths and weaknesses.' Lack of a well-differentiated self-concept may be 'normal' for an adolescent client's life stage, as adolescents are likely to be separating psychologically from their parents and developing an independent identity as adults (Erikson, 1971). However, many adults who come for career counselling also lack a clear self-concept. These clients often ask for help in assessing their talents and capabilities in order to be better equipped to make a decision about which career direction to pursue. Other clients present as not *liking* who they are. They believe that they know themselves, but suffer from low self-esteem and need help in increasing it.

Rational-emotive therapy has some useful frameworks to offer when considering career decision-making problems. Dryden (1979) states that, in his experience of career counselling, 'it is rare that a client is not subscribing to at least one of the irrational ideas outlined by Ellis (1962) that is relevant to his ability to make a career decision'. An example would be 'It is absolutely essential for me to reach the top in my chosen career; if I don't, it will be proof that I am a failure.'

Short-term solution-focused therapy offers some excellent tools to aid client decision making. One such tool is 'scaling'. Here is an example of how 'scaling techniques' may be used:

Career counsellor (Cc):	I'd like you to imagine a scale of 1–10, where 10 indicates that you are completely clear and decided about what you are going to do next and 1 shows that you are absolutely undecided. Where are you now on this scale?
Client (Cl):	Hmm ….. about 4 or 5.
Cc:	So what tells you you're at a 4 or 5 and not at 1?
Cl:	Well, I am pretty clear now about what I like and dislike, and what matters to me. I know what I don't want to do.
Cc:	OK, so if you moved up the scale a couple of points say, to 6 or 7, what would be in place then?
Cl:	I'd have narrowed down the field to a couple of areas to look into.
Cc:	What do you think needs to happen to achieve that …..?

This approach has a number of key points:

- It allows the client to determine his or her position on the scale.
- It focuses on resources and strengths already in place, not weaknesses and deficits.
- It moves from the general to the specific.
- It allows the individual the autonomy to set small steps towards achieving a future vision defined by the client.
- It defines success by observable differences, such as behaviour.

For further reading, see O'Connell (1998).

Other decision-making problems that may be uncovered during career counselling include:

- pressures from third parties (most frequently partners, parents or teachers) to follow a particular career direction;
- a conflict between two different parts of the self, for example, the creative self and the conventional self. Such a conflict may reflect values introjected (that is, accepted unquestioningly) from parents (see Chapter 4);
- fear of taking risks: it is better to have the self-image of a person who has the potential to be a success than to take the risk of trying but failing and therefore having the self-image of a failure;
- not taking responsibility for making decisions: people constantly seek advice from others, and therefore always have a convenient scapegoat if the advice works out badly for them;
- a conflict between career needs and personal needs. Women are particularly subject to pressures to marry and start a family, but clients of either gender may face problems in making career decisions because of conflicts between home/family needs and career needs; and
- fear of success operating simultaneously with a fear of failure, leading to paralysis.

Implications for career counsellors

The majority of clients who are having trouble making a career decision because they have no clear idea of their strengths and weaknesses can be helped through self-assessment exercises and the use of psychometric tests and other question-naires, as described in Chapters 4 and 5.

Often, just by identifying, acknowledging and discussing an irrational idea or an underlying conflict and thus becoming more aware of it, the client will be able to come to a resolution. Underlying conflicts can be brought to the surface and explored in more depth (see Chapter 4 on overcoming blocks).

Individual decision-making styles vary, with some clients preferring a logical and systematic approach and others adopting a more intuitive, 'it feels right' style. Exercises which the career counsellor can offer the client to assist with decision making are described in Chapter 6.

Particularly in the case of a dependent client who wants the career counsellor to take responsibility for making a decision, the contracting stage needs to be clearly negotiated and the client reminded of his or her responsibilities throughout the career counselling process (see Chapter 3).

A pattern of chronic indecisiveness which manifests itself not only in the arena of career decisions but throughout a client's life will require referral for personal counselling.

Problems in implementing a decision

> David had a PhD and had always seen his future career path in the academic world. However, there were very few vacancies, due to increasing competition for jobs in higher education, and he had made a number of applications for jobs, without success, over a period of two years.

Some clients come to career counselling with apparent clarity about what they want to do. A choice has been made; the problem presented is that for a number of possible reasons the choice cannot be implemented. These may include 'current economic conditions' and the state of the local job market.

Whatever the economic situation, it is inevitable that some people apply for jobs or for training and are rejected, either because they are considered unsuitable or because there is a limited number of opportunities. In times of recession, many more people will experience problems in implementing a career decision.

It is helpful to distinguish external from internal constraints. External con-straints are factors over which an individual has no control, for example, govern-ment economic policy or the fact that certain jobs are only to be found in specific locations. However, there is inevitably some 'internal' reason why people come to career counselling, otherwise they would modify their plans in the light of exter-nal circumstances. Internal constraints cover factors in an individual's personality, feelings or beliefs which act as a block to their career development. Most com-monly, when working with a client, the career counsellor will encounter an inter-relationship between both sets of factors, as David's case study demonstrates:

It emerged that David was feeling very angry and bitter towards a system which had, as he saw it, encouraged him to develop specialist skills and then had no use for them. The career counsellor encouraged him to express this frustration, and to think about the transferable skills which his research degree in a scientific subject gave him. David said that he had most enjoyed collecting and analysing data during his PhD studies. Questionnaires confirmed an orientation towards data rather than people; David was actually not at all motivated towards the teaching element of the posts for which he had been applying. He began to look at posts within the health service which required collecting and analysing medical statistics, and eventually found a job that suited him.

Other problems in implementing a career decision which may be encountered include:

- an unrealistic career aspiration;
- feelings of vulnerability due to previous experiences of rejection which lead a person to hold back from taking the risk of being rejected again;
- ineffective self-presentation, usually linked with poor self-esteem and/or lack of oral or written communication skills;
- discrimination (conscious or unconscious) in the employment market on the basis of age, gender, race, disability or social class;
- lack of financial resources to pursue appropriate training;
- the intervention of personal adversity in the form of an accident, illness or a bereavement, for example;
- a 'career ceiling' may have been reached; this tends to be common in mid-life, where opportunities for advancement within a particular career field become more limited; and
- an unrealistic wish to find a quick and painless 'fix'; people may need support to accept that it takes time and effort to make changes happen.

Implications for career counsellors

Experiences of rejection often give rise to very powerful feelings which need to be aired in career counselling before progress can be made in developing a plan of action for the future. For example, unresolved feelings, such as anger, about a previous rejection may complicate the process of coping with competitive recruitment procedures.

Problems in implementing a career decision arise frequently with people from 'minorities'. Some guidelines for the career counsellor in working with people who are at a disadvantage in the job market because of, for example, their gender, racial or social class origins are given in Chapter 8. Clients who have experienced discrimination and want to consider legal redress may need referral for specialist legal help.

The practical and emotional implications of personal adversity (such as a bereavement or divorce) may need to be worked through before the individual is able to implement a career plan, and referral for personal counselling may be appropriate.

The external circumstances which appear to be blocking the client should be explored. Some constraints are real, and the client will need to come to terms with them. Other 'external' constraints are more apparent than real, and may conceal an underlying internal conflict. Clients' apparent clarity about what they want to do should not be taken at face value. Sometimes clients who experience rejection are unconsciously 'sabotaging' themselves because they are ambivalent about their career choice, possibly because the career 'choice' was never actually their own.

Problems brought about by change in organisations

The kinds of change in an organisation that can cause people to come for career counselling (or be referred by their employer) include:

- the need to apply for a previously held job in a restructured department;
- a change in the nature of a job: for example, primary teaching involves much more administration than it used to;
- technological changes, such as the impact of new IT systems on jobs and skill requirements;
- downsizing, leading to increased pressure on resources and more demanding performance targets;
- change of boss: for example, to a person whose philosophy and/or personal style is incompatible;
- change in organisational values: for example, a greater emphasis may be placed on business acumen;
- the liquidation of a small business; and
- reorganisation, leading to job loss or redundancy.

Redundancy

Although there is less stigma attached to redundancy in the 21st century, it is still rather an unmentionable word, often clothed in euphemistic phrases such as 'The company has had to downsize', 'Your job has been deleted' or 'We'll have to let you go.' A person whose job has been made redundant may approach a career counsellor with a deep sense of shock, a feeling of shame, a reinforced impression of his or her own inadequacies, a strongly defiant reaction, or a sense of relief. Some people will actually say to the career counsellor 'I have been made redundant' because they *feel* redundant. The reality is that usually it is the job, not the individual, that has been made redundant.

The process of movement from one life situation (for example, employment) to another (for example, unemployment) involves coming to terms with loss, and the intense feelings of grief experienced after a redundancy can be similar to those felt by the bereaved. The degree of pain felt will depend on many individual factors, but perhaps the length of time with the employer, expectancy of re-employment, previous unresolved experiences of loss and the available financial and emotional support are the key ones. The following case studies illustrate how the 'same' event (reorganisation and subsequent 'deletion' of a person's job) can be experienced quite differently because of these individual factors:

Timothy had been in the accounts department of his company for 25 years. He was proud of working for his company, and he worked 'beyond the call of duty'. Since his partner died of cancer two years previously, he had been working even longer hours. He was 49 years old, and had an ageing mother to support. When he heard his job was 'surplus to requirements' after a reorganisation, he was very upset. In career counselling, it took several meetings for Timothy to work through his feelings of shock, panic and grief.

Jan was 41. She had been employed in her job as a researcher for 12 years. However, although she liked doing research, she had ceased to enjoy working for her employing organisation. She had a new boss for whom she had very little respect, and for the past year she had been considering leaving. She had few financial commitments, and good emotional support at home. When she heard her job was 'deleted' due to financial cutbacks, her first reaction was a deep sense of relief. In career counselling, although she addressed some feelings of bitterness (that her boss appeared not to value her skills), she was able to come to terms with the emotional impact very rapidly.

Implications for career counsellors

Unless clients are willing to acknowledge their feelings, early pressure may be placed on the career counsellor to provide a solution which provides the best job match, and to give training in job-hunting techniques. It is important for the career counsellor to be vigilant to the degree to which clients' negative feelings are getting in the way of a rational consideration of their present situation and future plans.

When career counselling clients who are experiencing any kind of change, it is helpful to have an understanding of the process of transition. Adams et al. (1976) define a transition as 'a discontinuity in a person's life space'. Smith (1989) has suggested a 'transition curve', depicting stages of emotional 'adjustment' to change (see Figure 2.1). The 'stages' are not time bound, and they may recur. For a discussion of the issues facing career counsellors working with clients experiencing change *within* an organisational context, see Chapter 7. See also Bridges (1995).

Shock, denial: Unable to believe that it has happened. 'You're joking!' A feeling of emptiness, perhaps numbness.

Euphoria: Making the best of it, and minimising the reality of the change. 'Now I've got time to … paint the house, take a holiday … – I didn't like the job anyway.'

Pining: Hoping that the job will come back – an unrealistic expectation that the next job will be exactly the same.

Anger: Blaming someone – 'I never could work with (my boss) anyway.' 'They should have …'

Guilt: Self-blame – 'They chose me because I wasn't up to it/did something wrong.'

Apathy: A sense of powerlessness and hopelessness as the reality sinks in.

Acceptance: Letting go of the past, and the emergence of a renewed optimism.

Future flows: Positive energy to move forward.

Figure 2.1   The transition curve

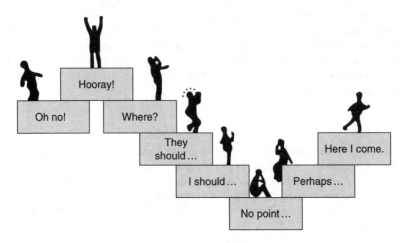

Source: Smith (1989)

For someone deeply or mildly affected by change, the career counsellor will need to use the skills of counselling to allow the client sufficient time to 'work through' some of the above feelings. For very depressed clients, a referral may be in order.

It is helpful for career counsellors to have an understanding that the loss of a job can mean a good deal more than the loss of pay and a set of tasks, although these are of course important. Other 'losses' include self-esteem, a social outlet and a structure to the day.

Performance-related problems

> Clifford felt a failure in his job as a sales representative. His sales figures were consistently lower than those of his colleagues, and at his appraisal he was told that he 'lacked drive'.

Problems related to performance are perhaps the most obvious kind to precipitate the need for a visit to a career counsellor. 'Career' has, after all, been traditionally associated with achievement, and a career counsellor may well be seen as someone able to get the individual back on the, temporarily interrupted, path to success.

There are two ways in which performance-related problems may come to light. Firstly, individuals may see themselves as having failed, or in a position where they might soon fail. Secondly, an employing organisation may have decided that an individual has, according to its requirements, failed. The two may or may not overlap. Box 2.3 lists some common presenting situations which may be linked to performance problems.

Box 2.3 Some performance-related presenting problems

- Dismissal
- Poor performance appraisal
- Failure to gain promotion after internal assessment
- Being 'passed over' for promotion in favour of a younger colleague
- Results consistently worse than those of colleagues
- Criticism from significant others (for example, parents, partners) for lack of achievement
- Continuing rejections on the job market
- 'Escaping' from failures by changing job/house/country
- Loss of motivation and effectiveness, which may arise because the person has reached a 'career plateau', perhaps through a lack of opportunities for career advancement.

At such times of perceived failure, feelings which may have lain dormant for years can surface. For example, long-time low self-esteem led Paul to inappropriate career choices in the desire to gain recognition from his father, who was incapable of showing any love for his son because of his own 'stiff upper lip' upbringing. Perfectionist values led Alice to accept from herself nothing but the best, even though she was performing very capably in most areas. As with redundancy, this 'sudden realisation' can come as a shock: 'I've never failed/had a poor assessment/been rejected before.'

Implications for career counsellors

As in the case of redundancy, the client's presenting feelings (for example, depression, demoralisation, anger, shame, panic) need to be acknowledged and addressed to some extent at least before it is possible to establish the nature of the problem, which may involve:

- a mismatch between a person's capabilities and the current job's demands. This might have led to poor performance through the onset of stress. Such poor performance may have arisen through the job being overly or insufficiently demanding. For example, boredom from understimulation can lead to stress, which can lead to loss of motivation and effectiveness (see Mulligan, 1988);
- a person's promotion path being blocked in a large organisation owing to a 'glass ceiling', a slimming down of available promotional opportunities, or a poor relationship with a significant manager;
- a deterioration of skills resulting from a failure to keep up with the demands of the current job; or
- a lack of real interest in the work itself, leading to lack of application and consequent poor performance.

Where clients' performance standards are in question, it may be beneficial to give a '360 degree feedback' exercise, to gain a relatively objective assessment of their strengths, weaknesses and development needs for the job. Additionally, a 'battery' of aptitude tests may reveal useful information about an individual's natural talents and capabilities (see Chapter 5). Where personality factors affect job performance, personality questionnaires can be illuminating, as in Clifford's case:

> Personality questionnaires revealed that Clifford was somewhat introverted, with a calm, even temperament and a thorough, patient approach to detail. Clifford recognised that he had been trying to succeed in an occupation for which he was temperamentally unsuited. He stopped trying to change himself, and instead changed his job from being a salesman to a 'behind the scenes' administrative support role.

The use of such tests and questionnaires must be undertaken with care – see Chapter 5 for a full discussion of their use in career counselling. In our approach, we prefer to offer a number of questionnaires and 'self-assessment exercises', rather than relying on just one or two of them. This approach leads to the identification of common themes, which clients value and find relevant.

Relationship problems

It may seem strange for a career counsellor to be approached about a relationship problem. Indeed, this is often not the presenting problem, but one that may emerge in counselling as a significant consideration. Justine's situation demonstrates how this can happen and markedly affect the direction of the career counselling.

> Justine was the director of a small company which had recently gone into liquidation. She approached career counselling ostensibly to 'check out' whether she was in the right career area. She had enjoyed her work, but her confidence had taken a knock. As the counselling progressed, she talked about how she tended to become over-involved with people at work. In particular, it was apparent that she had been depending too much on meeting her social needs through developing relationships with men with whom she worked closely. This led the career counsellor to focus with Justine not on appropriate occupations, but on the best work environment to safeguard against this happening again, the kind of social activities she could take up outside employment and whether to take personal counselling to look more closely at her underlying needs.

Thus, the problem presented to the career counsellor led to exploration at a deeper level. It might have been appropriate to explore alternative occupations, but in Justine's case this seemed less important than to work out ways of decreasing her reliance on so many of her needs being met through work.

The kind of relationship problems brought to career counselling include:

- someone having a continuing abrasive work relationship, or set of relationships;
- a manager finding it hard to motivate staff;
- a mid-career client only able to progress by taking on managerial responsibility, but having no experience and little confidence to do so;
- an employee finding it hard to accept the authority of a particular manager;
- someone who finds it hard to deal effectively with *anyone* in authority;
- a person low in self-esteem finding it hard to take criticism;
- a subordinate disappointed with his or her boss for lack of guidance; and
- someone experiencing an unusually strong sense of competition with peers, perhaps expressed through 'put-downs' at meetings.

Implications for career counsellors

Relationship problems may not necessarily be the ones put forward by clients early on in career counselling as issues they want to address. The contract initially agreed with the client may either have to be sufficiently broad, or be redefined as appropriate. This is a sensitive area, which may also require the skills of personal counselling. Positive outcomes may also be achievable through solution-focused coaching or therapy (O'Connell, 1998).

Career counsellors helping clients to deal with relationship problems can adopt a number of strategies. The use of personality and other questionnaires dealing with personal style may help clients to identify and 'own' their particular traits and style. Coaching in skills such as assertiveness and dealing with meetings through rehearsal and practice, may be possible within a career counselling contract, or a new coaching contract. Alternatively, a referral to an appropriately qualified counsellor or coach may be appropriate.

It is useful for career counsellors to appreciate some of the underlying issues associated with relationships at work, in particular, how people may recreate their relationships with parents or other significant figures when dealing with people at work. For example, a client who is disappointed with the lack of guidance he has received from his parents may express disappointment with his boss for lack of guidance. It may be possible to allow clients to see how their behaviour is linked in this way. For further exploration, a referral for personal counselling might be in order (see BACP Referral Directory). For a survey of psychodynamic approaches to counselling and career counselling, see Jacinto et al. (2000).

Expression and repression of creativity

What happens to the creativity encouraged in primary school when it is sometimes discouraged in those from the age of 14 upwards unless they are exceptionally talented? For example, those young people not taking art beyond the age of 14 may grow up believing that, since they are not apparently artistic, they are not creative. This is not necessarily the case, as it is possible to express creativity by, for example, innovation and development of an idea, project or product. Of course, this might take place in or out of work, or both.

The 'Protestant work ethic' is very strong, and many people see work as a very serious business, incompatible with the 'fun' element necessary in creativity. Creativity issues often emerge during mid-life. We often see clients who have so devoted themselves to doing well at work that they have sacrificed the expression of their creativity in all other parts of their lives. Alice's example, below, demonstrates how she sacrificed her creativity to please her father.

> Alice had worked for eight years in an accountancy firm. She had been successful, but the effects of stress had caused her to take time off. Through career counselling, she realised that she had been striving so hard for success to please her father, who had thoroughly approved of her promotions and increasing salary. Alice subsequently decided to seek work where she could combine her successful 'organised' self with her creative 'arty' side. Career counselling enabled her to realise the importance to her of this 'repressed' creativity, and also that she did not have to completely give up her organised self as well.

Implications for career counsellors

Clients who present to career counsellors as feeling bored, dull, grey and flat *may* be suffering from repressed creativity, the very part of them which represents vitality and energy. Somehow it has been suppressed, sapped or diverted. For those clients who are not able to realise, either partly or fully, their creativity through their work, it may be feasible to develop or revive a creative hobby outside employment.

The use of personality questionnaires and self-assessment exercises can be useful in highlighting clients' needs for expressing their creativity. The data produced from such exercises can give clients the confidence to 'do something about it'.

For people who want to express their creativity in their career, Dail (1989) is a helpful workbook, making use of imagery and fantasy techniques.

Summary

In this chapter we have discussed the issues which clients bring to career counselling in the belief that it can help career counsellors to show empathy and understanding if they can quickly recognise the common questions and dilemmas faced by their clients. However, we consider that it is important not to use this recognition to 'sum up' or 'pigeonhole' the client. Attention also needs to be given to differentiating 'presenting' from 'underlying' issues.

It is also important for career counsellors to recognise the limitations of their skills, experience and qualifications in order to make appropriate and timely referrals to other qualified psychotherapists, counsellors or coaches.

The problems clients bring and the underlying issues have been illustrated with case studies which give the flavour of career counselling in practice. The next four chapters examine the career counselling process in detail. Chapter 3 looks at the initial stages of screening, contracting and early exploration of the client's presenting problem.

Checklist: Issues brought to career counselling

☑ Be aware that concerns presented about 'career' may well be connected to non-work issues.

☑ Be sensitive to the possibility of any relevant underlying personal issues.

☑ It is often possible to do 'good enough' work with clients without unravelling underlying issues; career counsellors need to respect clients' right to privacy.

☑ Make every attempt to let clients know, before and during career counselling, that you have some empathy with the kind of issues they are facing.

☑ Avoid pigeonholing any client as 'typical' – there will always be an individual and unique response to any situation.

☑ Recognise that clients often come to career counselling believing they *ought* to be different from the way they are.

☑ Remember that feelings of failure and confusion may be influenced by parental expectations.

☑ Be conscious that a person's life or work values may, or may not, change according to their 'life stage' or as a response to key life events.

☑ Be prepared to adapt your counselling approach to that of the client.

☑ If a client is having difficulty implementing a decision, be prepared to consider internal, as well as external, constraints.

3 Screening, Contracting and Exploring

It is important for the career counsellor to be concerned with what happens *before* the first counselling meeting because it can have a profound effect on the career counselling relationship. The stages of screening and contracting are actually part of constructing a relationship with any client, and have particular relevance to the role and expectations of a *career* counsellor.

Screening is a process which usually occurs before the counsellor and client contract to meet. It enables the counsellor to gather information about the prospective client, and the client to gain information about the counsellor and the service provided. Such information can assist both to decide whether to proceed further.

Contracting is a process by which counsellor and client come to a clear understanding about working methods and their respective roles in the career counselling. Sometimes screening may take place during the initial contracting phase, as the counsellor and client may, as yet, be less than fully committed.

As we made clear in the introductory chapter, in career counselling the responsibility for decision making lies with the client. Clients may not, however, be prepared or ready to undertake this responsibility. There may be a continuing expectation that the career counsellor should be able to guide the client into the 'right' career (see Box 1.2 (p. 9) f or a description of client responsibilities during career counselling). This implies that clients need to be sufficiently 'ready' in order to get the best from career counselling. It is therefore important to contract with people to ensure maximum readiness to work with a counselling, rather than an advice, approach. People may not necessarily prefer an advisory approach; they may simply not know that 'counselling' can be effective – so the screening and contracting stages of the career counselling process are in themselves educative.

Screening and contracting are of course inextricably linked. By responding to statements of what career counselling can and cannot do, clients can make an informed decision whether to contract in or out.

This chapter addresses considerations about structuring a career counselling service, and how potential clients can be encouraged to approach career counselling in an active, as opposed to a passive, state of mind. The nature of clients' expectations is discussed. The contracting that takes place face to face in the first meeting during the exploration of the client's presenting problem and throughout the career counselling process is subsequently tackled.

Screening

Screening in writing
A well-written document, in paper form or online, for prospective clients will help to minimise misunderstandings about what a career counselling service can offer.

A prospectus, leaflet or brochure has a number of purposes:

- *Educative*   Prospective users of a service may not know of this kind of approach to career counselling. Writing down what is expected of clients sets out what the contract involves and educates at the same time. Those people who feel uncertain whether or not they can comply with these expectations can choose to ask further questions, either on the telephone, via email or in person (see following sections). This can help to clarify their thinking and perhaps increase trust in what may be an unfamiliar process.
- *Contractual*   By stating what the service can and cannot do, and what is expected of clients, the terms of an offer are being set out. Having a written document increases the chances that a client will have 'taken in' what the contract means. This is preferable to leaving matters open to the vagaries of telephone discussions, referrals and recommendations.
- *Information giving*   Written information can and should accurately reflect the services offered. It should include details of the nature of the service, the qualifications of the counsellors, the professional ethical codes practised, and details of any other facilities such as libraries, referral resources and job-hunting support and coaching.
- *Trust building*   Stating clearly what is on offer reduces any opportunity for unrealistic expectations. Written information can create a certain 'image' of a service which, hopefully, is comprehensive, caring and professional. This in itself lays the foundations for building trust, by initially addressing clients' concerns.

Screening on the telephone

A telephone conversation is more personal than a written document. Voice contact can do much to build up (or undermine) trust. Adequate time and human resources are necessary in order to operate telephone screening effectively.

Questions and concerns can be dealt with prior to commitment to any meeting. Information which might be useful should the person choose to become a client can be revealed by eliciting:

- the source of the referral, and consequent expectations; for example, 'You saw my colleague/friend/partner and were very helpful';
- the urgency of the situation; for example, 'I have to decide whether to stay or leave the organisation within a month'; and
- the inquirer's initial perception of what a career counselling service can offer; for example, 'I've been working abroad for five years and have no idea how to approach the UK job market'.

In telephone screening it is possible to give and receive feedback and fulfil the educative, contracting and, particularly, the trust-building functions of screening mentioned already. Information can of course be given, but this may be more easily absorbed in written form. A subsequent discussion, either on the telephone or in person, can reinforce and expand on the information given in writing and deal with further questions.

Screening in person

Face-to-face introductory meetings with a group of potential clients are an effective way of increasing the realism of expectations. This does not require commitment on either side. Such meetings are (a) economical – you can say the same words to several prospective clients at the same time; (b) more 'personal' than written or telephone communications; and (c) real – they show that you exist, who you are, what the place is like physically and can give a sense of the way you work.

At our 'open meetings', people often start off by saying that they are looking for advice, or that they want to be 'put on the right path'. These may be the socially acceptable words to use – it is harder to ask for help directly or to demand something less tangible and obvious, such as 'someone to listen to me'. It may also be easier to justify the time and money to interested third parties if you end up with a tangible written report or even a new career! One of the aims of the open meeting is to put over the service as one offering counselling and not advice, to encourage clients to take an active, rather than passive, approach.

We find that clients who come to open meetings leave better informed about what the process entails, and about their role and responsibility as a client. If they decide to proceed, they are better prepared psychologically for career counselling. In addition, they have resolved many of the their minor concerns – such as 'How do I get there?' or 'Where do I park?' – by practical experience. Clients are therefore likely to be less nervous and uncertain about what the place will be like when they arrive.

Perhaps because of this initial work, we have found that the trust level is higher at the beginning of the counselling than with clients who have only read written information.

Open meetings can also give useful information to the counsellor. For example:

- What has been the person's experience of any previous career help?
- What are the person's experiences and expectations of tests and questionnaires?
- Has the person had current or past experience of psychotherapy or counselling?
- What is the person's level of pain or distress, and readiness, for career counselling?

The last point raises the question of whether and how to discourage people who are unlikely to benefit from the career counselling process, and the need for appropriate sources of referral. Usually people screen themselves out. Occasionally, however, we have to discourage people. We would always try to suggest an alternative source of help if a personal issue seemed to be more prominent than the career problem, or if the counsellor judged the client's expectations to be too unrealistic to work with.

There is often an overlap between career, personal and skills development issues. Again, communicating with clarity about what is and is not on offer, and what the service aims to provide, will help clients decide whether this is a suitable service for them.

Written preparation by client

Some kind of written preparation by clients is another way of encouraging a more active approach to the career counselling process. It can also enable them, before the first meeting, to decide to screen themselves out, and is a test of their commitment. We ask clients to complete a 'background questionnaire', and to write briefly about their perceived strengths and weaknesses. A few suggestions of appropriate questions or issues to ask clients to write about are given in Box 3.1.

Box 3.1 Suggestions for written preparation

- Biodata (name, address, telephone, age, marital status etc.)
- Education and career details
- Aspects of education, training and career enjoyed/disliked
- Aspects of education and training good/poor at
- Details of non-career achievements
- Occupations of family, partner
- Occupations considered
- Hobbies and interests
- Self-assessment of strengths and weaknesses in career
- Description of current situation
- Idea of kind of help sought from the career counselling

There is a big difference between clients who have and have not completed some written work prior to the first meeting. As one ex-client said: 'The introductory homework can only be done with thought – you put yourself at a disadvantage without doing the preparation. You don't arrive at the first meeting with a completely blank mind, expecting to be led by the hand through the process. You have done some pretty hard reflection.'

Contracting

The question of money: who pays and for what?

If the career counsellor works for an independent, fee-paying service, the question of money arises. Clients either pay for themselves, or are sponsored by an interested third party, perhaps their employer.

When a client pays a fee, this may affect his or her expectations of 'value'. Value may be seen in terms of a tangible end-product, an 'after' state which can be shown to others as having been influenced by the counselling. But clients do not just commit themselves financially. They give time (a good deal of it in the case of many clients), both during and between meetings, and a willingness to participate actively in, rather than just passively 'attend', career counselling.

The issue of money is significant. It probably encourages the client to take contracting prior to commitment more seriously. The questions being addressed include:

- What will I be getting for my money? Will it be worth it?
- How will I justify the expenditure, given my other commitments?
- Can I and do I want to afford this now?

Where possible, we do encourage clients who are earning, to pay at least a proportion of the fees themselves. This increases, though never guarantees, the likelihood of commitment. We always insist that the individual actually attending career counselling is financially responsible for any missed appointments.

If an interested third party is paying, there may be an extra expectation which needs to be addressed, or at least acknowledged. With all clients, but particularly in the case of third-party referrals, the question of confidentiality must be addressed.

Confidentiality and third-party referrals

As in any counselling, it is assumed that confidentiality will be offered and maintained by the counsellor and any staff who have access to client files. While confidentiality is an ideal, and its maintenance enhances trust and openness, it may be easier to achieve when career counselling is offered independently of the organisation. See Chapter 7, 'Career Counselling in Organisations', for a discussion of employer-sponsored referrals.

Sometimes we see 'younger people' who have essentially been 'sent', and usually paid for, by one or both parents. We always try to ensure that such clients make their own appointments and have read our literature. This, however, is not always possible, and particular attention must be paid to explaining in the first meeting what the career counselling process involves and what is expected from the client. If this is not done, there is a danger that a client's lack of commitment could well manifest itself in non-attendance and last-minute cancellations.

Occasionally, a parent will ring up and express a concern about how the counselling is proceeding. We are usually happy to offer a little time to concerned parents, being clear that it is the parent who then becomes the client. Listening skills can be used and counselling support given, but the content of the daughter's or son's career counselling will not be revealed. There has been one occasion when a parent, fully respecting the confidentiality contract and recognising his own needs, booked a session for himself! The following example demonstrates how we responded to a concerned parent, for the benefit of everyone concerned.

Helena was 22 years old and had worked with animals since she left school, but wanted a change as there were no further prospects. Her father (Mr Vaughan) had obtained a brochure and phoned up to book her in for career counselling. The member of staff who took his call explained how the service operated, and suggested that his daughter read the brochure and then book the appointments herself.

At the contracting stage, it was clear that Helena was there for herself and committed to the counselling process. The counsellor enquired about Helena's relationship with her father. Helena said that he had always been very supportive and that, although he was paying for the sessions, he wasn't pushing her in a particular direction. The counsellor also clarified the confidentiality agreement, and made it clear that Helena (and not the counsellor) was responsible for giving any feedback to her father.

As the career counselling progressed, Helena's lack of knowledge of the world of work became apparent, and the counsellor explained that Helena could use the careers library to inform herself about various possible career options. Helena set off with enthusiasm to find out more about careers.

(Continued)

(Continued)

Before the final meeting was scheduled, Mr Vaughan phoned up and spoke to a member of the support staff. Sounding very anxious, he said that his daughter needed her horizons broadened because she had been working in such a limited field, and he wanted the counsellor to give Helena a range of suggestions of suitable careers. The member of staff listened, and then explained to Mr Vaughan that clients, together with the support of the career counsellor, are involved in generating career ideas.

At Helena's final meeting, she was not ready to make a final decision about her choice of career, but drew up a shortlist of careers to investigate in more detail. At the end of the session, the counsellor asked Helena how she would be giving feedback to her father, and Helena said she had arranged to have lunch with him. She said she thought he would be pleased because, even though she had not reached a final decision, her horizons were now much broader!

Here we see that, by using a trained member of staff (*not* the counsellor) to talk to the parent, the counsellor was not pressured in any direct way to defend the approach offered. In this situation, as in many others, the parent may have been using the career counselling to give his daughter the kind of attention he would like to have given her himself, but could not. The telephone call was one way of reassuring himself that this was happening.

Screening and contracting in the first meeting

However much information a client may have had beforehand, the first meeting with the career counsellor is the time to establish and confirm the contract with the client. If someone else has been involved in arranging career counselling on a client's behalf, this is the time to test out the client's own commitment to the process.

From reading any written preparation, and during the first meeting, the counsellor can glean a good deal about the client's commitment. It may also be possible, through discussion and appropriate questioning, to discover any destructive patterns of behaviour which the client may be bringing into the counselling relationship. For example, a client who has a feeling of constantly being let down may unconsciously 'sabotage' the career counselling.

Essentially, we are asking ourselves whether this is the right place, at the right time, and with the right counsellor – for this client. A difficulty may arise when it is clear that there are personal issues which need addressing before a career decision can be made. It may be that all a client can bear to admit to at the time is the career issue, and the need for counselling is expressed as a desire for career counselling (that is, *not* ongoing personal counselling or psychotherapy). 'Going for career counselling' sounds more socially acceptable than 'going for therapy'. It has a clear structure and aim which clients can talk about more easily with their partner, family or friends. Once they have arrived in the career counselling room, clients may want to use some of the counselling time for discussing deeper issues.

After all, what is 'career' or 'employment' other than what people choose to *be* for a good proportion of their lives, particularly in terms of achievement, success, recognition and the attainment of compatible values?

A crucial consideration in the contracting stage is that, although we are contracting with clients about objectives which are to do with the career 'externals' (for example, 'Should I stay with or leave medicine?'), we are aware at the same time of possible internal agendas concerning thoughts and feelings (for example, 'I have decided to leave medicine – I want support during this "letting go" phase'). Such issues raise the question of the boundary between career and personal counselling.

Boundaries between career and personal counselling

As career counsellors, we are offering a range of possible services, as listed in Box 1.1 (p. 6). We are not offering long-term or ongoing personal counselling contracts.

We are aiming to establish a collaborative or 'adult-to-adult' relationship, not a 'parent–child' one. Cochran (1997) refers to the client as 'agent', not 'patient'. We find it helpful to liken the career counselling process to a journey. For example: 'This is where you are now. There's a place that you might want to get to; in between there is a journey. Our meetings are only part of your journey. Very few people get to their destination by the last meeting here. But you should travel some way down the road.' This gives licence to the client to accept the career counselling as a process, and feel less obliged to seek an answer by the final meeting. It also encourages clients to take responsibility for making their journey a productive one, and therefore to be fully motivated to complete 'home' assignments (see Chapter 4).

However effective a screening process has been, very occasionally a person whose degree of distress is so strong that this collaborative, adult-to-adult career counselling is unlikely to be effective will 'slip through the net' and arrive for a first meeting. As in any form of counselling, the decision about whether or not to take on a client for career counselling must be based on ethical considerations, the level of rapport (although this of course can change) and the counsellor's professional judgement about whether the counselling will be of value to this client *now*. Referral may be required. As most counsellors realise, making a referral is a delicate skill, and can always be perceived at some level as a rejection. (See also pp. 125–7)

If a client is in psychotherapy, does the psychotherapist know that the client is having career counselling? If not, why not, and what are the implications? Could the career counsellor be misused as an alternative therapist? We advise clients to let their therapist know they are attending career counselling. Again, this helps to set the boundaries of the counselling. One advantage of working with clients familiar with counselling or psychotherapy is their awareness of the 'counselling' (not advice) nature of the contract. A disadvantage is that they can easily slip into 'therapy mode'. This can be minimised by reminding the client, when appropriate, of the *career* aspect of the counselling contract. These 'boundary' issues are explored further in Chapter 8.

Number, length and frequency of meetings

Whatever way the career counselling is structured, it is important that clients are briefed accordingly. This is always true, but perhaps especially so in the case of single consultations, where clients may expect to be given advice on the best career. Briefing can be in the form of a concise note which reflects, in tone and content, the nature of the service offered and the contribution expected of both the counsellor and the client.

Number of meetings

Flexibility is vital, fitting the service provided to the needs of the client, rather than the reverse. This means that the career counsellor should always be prepared to re-contract, if the need arises. There may, for example, be a need for more exploratory work, or further work on self-presentation. However, we have found that a programme of four or five meetings is about right for the majority of people.

If tests are administered, meetings can be structured as follows:

- *1st visit:* contracting, exploring (1 ½ hours);
- *2nd visit:* questionnaires and tests (2–6 hours);
- *3rd visit:* feedback and discussion of home assignments and questionnaire/test results (2 hours);
- *4th visit:* discussion of reflections and home assignments, brainstorming ideas, discussing realism of ideas, information on ideas, agreeing research and action plan (1 ½ hours);
- *5th visit:* review of progress, coaching and rehearsal in job hunting (1 ½ hours).

If tests or questionnaires are not used, fewer meetings may be needed. In either case, it is useful to contract for a specified number of meetings: having an endpoint in sight can sometimes galvanise a client into a ready state for 'moving on to the next stage', which might, for example, be a preparedness to carry out research into one or two careers. Career counsellors, with appropriate training and skills, should also be prepared to renegotiate the number and timing of meetings, particularly if a personal or developmental issue emerges in the process of counselling which requires further time or a different emphasis. The possibility of a referral to a personal counsellor or coach should also be considered.

The frequency of meetings may, but should not necessarily, be influenced by the urgency with which clients need to make a career decision (frequency of meetings may also be affected by more practical factors, such as the distance the client has to travel). A gap of at least three or four days between meetings allows time for reflection and the completion of home assignments. The gap may be longer further on in the career counselling process, as the client may need to progress with some practical research before returning for a 'review' meeting (see Chapter 6).

Single consultations

A single consultation can be of benefit if the client has a fairly clear self-concept and a reasonable level of self-esteem and, prior to the meeting, undertakes some written preparation. Some clients will need little more than a single discussion on setting career goals, the strategy of job hunting or where and how to find relevant occupational information. Other occasions when a single consultation may suffice or be preferable include situations where:

- the client is on the brink of a decision, and wants a single meeting to clarify his or her thinking;
- the client wants to access occupational information – a single meeting might help to gain the confidence needed to do so;
- time is at a premium – a single meeting, together with written preparation, may help give some structure to thoughts, feelings and ideas.

In most cases, however, we believe that much more can be gained from a series of counselling meetings, combined with the use of various questionnaires and self-assessment exercises.

Setting objectives at the contracting stage

Establishing some objectives provides structure for both the client and the counsellor, and can be a basis for a subsequent review of progress. Any objectives set should not become a straitjacket, but should merely provide a general framework for the counselling. Getting a client to say something like 'I want to be more clear about my career strengths and weaknesses' encourages ownership, an emphasis on process, and a career focus. A more specific objective might be 'I want to understand why I can't hold down a job for more than six months' or 'I want to decide between moving to a generalist management role or remaining within my specialism.'

Typical client objectives are listed in Box 3.2.

Box 3.2 Objectives for career counselling

- I want to decide on my next career step.
- I want to decide whether to change career or employer.
- I want to improve my job-hunting techniques and maintain self-esteem while I am unemployed.
- I want to decide whether to go for a general management or partner position, or develop my specialist skills further.
- I want to decide whether or not to return to full-time education.
- I want to increase my awareness and knowledge of the requirements for success in several occupations.
- I want to consider my suitability for self-employment.
- I want to develop an outline career plan for the next five years.
- I want to decide whether to continue to tertiary education, to train via employment or have a 'gap year'.

Some clients are less concerned to make a career *decision* ('Should I follow path x or y?') than to have support in dealing with a career-related issue. This may be about coming to terms with a loss, such as redundancy, not being promoted, coping with a new boss, or the increased financial pressure of a spouse/partner re-entering education. If the emphasis that emerges is more on managing a difficult relationship, coaching may be beneficial.

It is also possible that the client's initial objectives are misguided in some way, and here, too, the counsellor should remain flexible enough to alter the contract appropriately, as the following case study demonstrates.

> George had been a moderately successful musician. But, over the past few years, his engagements had been reduced to the point where he had to take on alternative employment. Through his girlfriend, he had obtained work as a 'librarian/researcher' for a photographic agency. He approached career counselling, attended an open meeting, and booked in for a series of sessions. In his written preparation, he expressed a desire to be informed of specific openings available in his field. He enjoyed, and was praised for, his work, and wanted to continue in this direction, but could see no future or security in his present employment. With a steady relationship, and a currently stable income, he wanted to build for the future. It soon became clear that his expectations of career counselling were unrealistic and, since he knew what he wanted to do, there were other issues to address. He knew little about training opportunities in librarianship or information work and felt very unsure about how to approach job hunting. The counsellor redefined the contract to this end, giving him access to appropriate information, helping him to develop an appropriate CV and providing interview practice.

In this instance it became necessary for the career counsellor to combine counselling skills with information-giving and even teaching, demonstrating and coaching skills.

The influence of tests on client expectations

Client perceptions about psychometric testing need to be explored during contracting. Many people are aware that psychometric tests are used to assess people for jobs. They may also be aware of their usage in career guidance, where a 'test and tell' approach may have been adopted – the client is 'assessed' and a short interview provides a basis for the consultant, usually an occupational psychologist, to advise on careers commensurate with the test results.

In counselling, it is vital that any use of psychometric tests and other questionnaires should serve, rather than dominate, the counselling relationship. Test 'results' can be used as a basis for discussion, the evaluation of self-perceptions and a way of addressing feelings concerning performance. At best, such results are only a guide, and any written or face-to-face screening and contracting should emphasise this fact. Clients may need to be reminded that tests will not be used to 'select' them for a particular occupation. This can help to remove any potential confusion between this *counselling* meeting and previous *selection* interviews.

Another consideration when contracting is that the client may be affected by feelings about past tests, examinations and other performance-related experiences. If the influence of these feelings is very strong, it may be wise to leave out any testing altogether, or at least postpone it until a later meeting when the client feels more secure. See Chapter 5 for a fuller discussion on the use of tests and questionnaires in career counselling.

Exploration

The process of contracting already described is inextricably linked with the process of exploration. During the first meeting, it helps if the counsellor bears the following tasks in mind:

- building rapport to enable the client to discuss their concerns freely;
- helping the client to explore and clarify what and who have influenced career and educational choices; and
- exploring any written preparation undertaken by the client.

Building rapport

As in any counselling relationship, there is a great deal which can be done to build rapport and trust quickly, and enable clients to talk freely. This may, to some extent, have been done through the earlier contracting, particularly if the client has been to an introductory meeting. However, most clients tend to arrive feeling fairly nervous and uncertain of what will happen. The counsellor's job at this stage is largely to enable clients to talk as easily as possible about themselves.

The *physical setting* is important. It will help if the 'tone' of the office is friendly, the chairs of similar type and with no barriers, such as a desk, between counsellor and client. If it is specifically career counselling which is being offered, a few work-related magazines on a small table might be useful if clients are kept waiting.

It may be helpful (for the counsellor) and interesting (for the client) to hang a quotation on the wall which encapsulates some aspect of the philosophy of career counselling. Ours is a quote from Nelson Mandela's 1994 inaugural speech:

> "Our deepest fear is not that we are inadequate. Our deepest fear is that we are powerful beyond measure. It is our light, not our darkness, that most frightens us. We ask ourselves, who am I to be brilliant, gorgeous, talented and fabulous? You are a child of God. Your playing small doesn't serve the world. There is nothing enlightening about shrinking so that other people won't feel insecure around you. We are born to make manifest that glory of God within us. It is not just in some of us, it's in everyone. And as we let our light shine, we unconsciously give other people permission to do the same. As we are liberated from our own fear, our presence automatically liberates others."

Career counselling requires all the basic counselling skills of listening, responding with respect and empathy, asking open questions and summarising, which have been well documented elsewhere (Egan, 2002). Allowing the client to tell his or her 'story' will, in itself, increase rapport. An open question to begin the meeting, such as 'What made you decide on career counselling at this point in your life?', will usually encourage the client to talk freely. In addition, it is possible to pick up some information which may be useful later in the career counselling. Box 3.3 suggests a number of questions for first meetings.

Box 3.3 Suggested questions for first meeting

Issue	Question
Was the client personally recommended?	How did you hear of us? Why did you choose this service?
What are the client's expectations?	What do you hope to gain from career counselling?
How is the counselling valued by the client? Are there any third-party expectations?	What made you decide on career counselling at this point in your life? (A useful opening question.)
Has the client received any previous career help?	What kind of career help have you had in the past? [For example,] At the age of 16 did you have any help in choosing options? Who influenced your choices? (Ditto for other choice points.)
What is the general emotional state of the client? Is 'career' the presenting problem?	What issues in your life concern you at the moment? What else is happening?
Is the client receiving personal counselling or other support?	What supports do you have at the moment?
What are the client's expectations of testing and questionnaires?	How do you expect tests and questionnaires might be able to help?

Exploring influences on career and educational choices

Exploring how the client has made career decisions in the past at major choice points (selecting options at school; decision about first job; decisions about changing jobs), including decisions to turn *down* a job offer, can assist the career counsellor in formulating hunches about the degree to which the client has taken responsibility for decision making and follow-through in the past.

Kathy came to career counselling because her first year as an accountancy trainee had been a miserable one, and she had been confused about her career direction for some time. Her teachers had told her what subjects to study, and her parents had told her to take a degree in business studies because she would be able to get a good job. At college, all her friends went on to study accountancy, so Kathy followed suit. She had never taken responsibility for a single career decision.

Exploring any early ideas the client may have had as a child or adolescent and what happened to them can be helpful at this stage. Unfulfilled career ambitions or special interests might still be resurrected in some form. The client may need to express feelings (possibly of loss) associated with unfulfilled dreams, as the following case study shows:

> At the first career counselling meeting Alex appeared depressed and flat. The question 'What did you want to do when you grew up?' revealed that he had loved drawing and painting as a child, but in secondary school he was told that his art was not good enough to make a success of it commercially. A flood of emotion poured out. He was near to tears as he confessed that he had never drawn or painted since, and expressed bitter resentment about the advice he had been given to train in banking instead. Several meetings later, Alex reported that he had enrolled in an evening class in art.

Both Kathy and Alex felt little control over influencing the direction of their work choices. Career counselling helped Alex to realise his strength of feeling about his lack of *self-efficacy*, and increase it. Self-efficacy was defined by Bandura (1977) as the extent to which a person believes that he or she can perform the behaviour required in any given situation.

Exploring written preparation

The first meeting is also the appropriate time to go through the client's written preparation, over which he or she may have taken considerable trouble.

Certain clients will have found the process of completing any written preparation both challenging and illuminating This can help to create the right 'climate' for exploring a topic further.

> Ginny had spent several hours preparing for her first career counselling meeting. She admitted to her career counsellor that she had not addressed such questions for many years. She had noticed some clear patterns in what she enjoyed doing at school and university, but was not doing now.

Clients may also signpost their difficulties very clearly in the written preparation. This usually signals readiness to explore the topic:

> Under the section on health in her preparation questionnaire, Heather wrote 'severe arthritis'. During the first meeting, it emerged that she had been a successful (and happy) nursery nurse, but she was unable to continue to work with children because of the disabling effects of arthritis in her hands. Subsequent counselling focused on her feelings of frustration and loss. This was a necessary stage in a process of 'letting go' in preparation for changing direction.

Some clients are, quite naturally, more reticent about exposing very personal information in writing before they have met the counsellor, and rapport will need to be good before such information is divulged:

> Although he did not mention it in his written preparation, Danny had been supporting his partner, who eventually died of AIDS. Through their contact with AIDS counsellors, Danny became interested in counselling as a career, and wanted to assess his suitability for it.

Sometimes helpful information can emerge from exploring any gaps or discrepancies in the information presented:

> The counsellor noticed that Michael had missed out a whole year of his life in his 'background questionnaire'. Exploration of this gap revealed that he had been asked to leave after the first year of a course at agricultural college, and brought out his acute feelings of embarrassment about failing in his father's eyes (he came from a long line of farmers).

Using the clues raised by clients' behaviour

An important counselling skill is to take note of any ways in which clients reproduce in their career counselling the very emotions, attitudes and behaviour causing them difficulty in their lives. Clients often give hints about these issues, not through what they say directly, but in a very vivid manner through the way they behave.

Being able to establish the nature and source of the initial referral can be an invaluable source of information about the client's issues and their relationship to career counselling. Did they hear of you from someone yesterday, and want a meeting tomorrow? Or did they ring up, request a brochure, and sit on it for a year before making an appointment, which they then cancelled at the last minute, before booking again? Were they recommended? If so, by whom? By an ex-client who said the career counselling 'changed his life'? Or by a counsellor, psychotherapist, coach or GP? Did they find you on a listing, in the Yellow Pages or on the Internet? Have they researched several counselling services in a thorough and systematic way? Clients also show something of their personalities and problems through the way they make appointments. Are they quick and businesslike? Or tentative and long-winded? The following case study demonstrates how the manner in which the meetings were arranged gave the career counsellor some important clues concerning Tina's problem:

The brother of this client originally booked in himself for career counselling. Ten days before his initial appointment, he telephoned to say that both he and his sister Tina would like to attend an open meeting. He said he was uncertain if he needed the career counselling, but his sister might. At the open meeting, he made it clear he would like to 'hand over' his appointments lock, stock and barrel to his sister. 'Don't worry,' he said, 'I can give her all the preparation forms.' He hardly allowed her to speak at all in making the arrangements for *her* meetings! The counsellor making the appointments made sure that she received a brochure of her own, new preparation papers and a fresh letter of confirmation.

In the counselling meetings, it turned out that the issue of 'independence vs. conformity' was a crucial one for her, as was the matter of being able to achieve her power as a woman! Tina expected to be 'told' of the best career solution (she was used to authority figures making decisions for her), until it was established in the first meeting that she could use the career counselling service as a way of discovering herself, as her counsellor had no vested interest in persuading her to move in a particular direction.

Another useful pointer is the counsellor's own feelings towards the client:

Kathy's counsellor found at the first meeting that she was strongly tempted to respond in a maternal fashion towards Kathy. These feelings were unusual for this counsellor, and her hunch that important issues to be tackled in the counselling included Kathy's dependency needs and her avoidance of taking responsibility for making her own decisions turned out to be accurate.

The counsellor's feelings should act as no more than the basis of a hunch or hypothesis to be checked out later. Such feelings may reflect something in the counsellor, rather than in the client.

The whole-person approach

As we have seen, clients can bring one or several issues to career counselling. There is potential for confusion between personal and career counselling, not least because there can be a very real connection between the two. In the following case it would have been impossible and unproductive to attempt to explore career issues without considering the context of the client's life as a whole:

Nina was from Cyprus, and nearing the end of a second degree course when she came for career counselling. She was being pressured by her family to marry a particular man, about whom she had strong doubts; she liked him as a friend but

(Continued)

(Continued)

did not see him as a potential husband. In the first meeting, it emerged that she had been continuing with her studies as a way of avoiding making difficult decisions, concerning career and marriage. Now that her time as an 'academic' was coming to an end, she had no choice but to address these decisions.

The career counsellor needs flexibility to move back and forth between all matters of concern to a client, whilst recognising that the central focus should remain the career issues. If personal issues threaten to overwhelm the career counselling process, a referral for personal counselling may be necessary (see Figure 1.1 on p. 3).

Summary

Effective screening and contracting lay a sound foundation for subsequent career counselling. The career counsellor needs to be alert from the point of first contact to issues which, if left unresolved, may have the power to sabotage the whole process.

The kind of contracting which is necessary will depend on a number of considerations, including clients' readiness for career counselling and their experience of counselling as a process. There is inevitably a different starting point for each individual. Once counselling has begun, however, it is necessary to keep a careful watch on clients' commitment, and whether the contract needs readdressing. Contracting is like a thread running through the whole career counselling process.

We have also discussed the structure of first meetings and important topics for the client to explore. During this phase, clients will begin to clarify their interests, skills and values. The counsellor will need to be alert to underlying themes and be aware of hunches or hypotheses about the client, the problem and any likely outcomes, as these may be helpful to pursue at the next stage of the career counselling process.

In the following chapter, the next stage is discussed: enabling clients to develop a clearer understanding of themselves in relation to the world of work. This is the heart of the career counselling process. Chapter 4 examines the questions the client needs to address at this stage, and describes several exercises which can assist the client in addressing them.

Checklist: Screening, contracting and exploring

☑ It is vital to agree with clients on clear and attainable objectives for the career counselling.

☑ Agree with clients on your and their responsibilities to achieve the agreed objectives.

☑ Be prepared to 're-contract' with clients as appropriate.

(Continued)

(Continued)

☑ Communicate clearly through writing, telephone and face-to-face discussion the nature and scope of the service on offer.

☑ Note that the degree of confidentiality offered will affect the openness and efficacy of career counselling.

☑ Be alert to the possible need for referral for personal counselling, or other sources of help.

☑ Offer a 'flexible framework' when establishing the number, length and frequency of meetings.

☑ Whilst being 'non-judgemental', formulate hunches about what might be going on for a client.

☑ Explore past educational and career decisions with sensitivity.

☑ Be aware of a client's commitment to the career counselling by checking out the nature and source of referral to you.

☑ Take into account the client's 'whole life' context.

4 Enabling Clients' Understanding

At the first meeting clients will have begun to tell the counsellor their perceptions of themselves and their career situation. Whether the problem presented and explored in the first meeting is a relatively straightforward one of making a client more aware of their career strengths and weaknesses, or a more complex one of, for example, addressing feelings of loss and anger after redundancy, clients are usually seeking, implicitly or explicitly, clarification and self-understanding in the following areas:

- Who am I? Where am I now?
- What do I want? Where do I want to be?
- What are the resources within and around me that can enable me to move on?
- What is stopping me from moving on?

The client's own answers to these questions may be inaccurate, distorted or limited in various ways. One of the tasks of this stage is to help clients to develop a more objective and accurate self-understanding and deepen their insight into their situation. The aim is to enable clients to move towards a new and more constructive perspective which can form a basis for decision and action.

In this chapter we will look at the use of home assignments between meetings. Like the preparation work clients undertake before the first meeting, exercises to encourage exploration and clarification can prove powerful. We will discuss the purposes of between-session assignments, give some examples of the types of exercise which can be given to clients, and explain how to make use of them as an integral part of the career counselling process. A summary of these exercises is also given in Appendix H. We will also look at ways of responding to, and challenging, clients' inner blocks to moving forward within career counselling meetings.

For some clients, greater self-understanding is all that is needed, and this may promote renewed energy or a change of attitude. For others, self-understanding is just the first stage. They want career counselling to help them make decisions or formulate action plans; this stage is addressed in Chapter 6.

Using home assignments

Any home assignment has a number of general purposes, whilst each assignment will have its own specific purposes, relating to that particular exercise.

General purposes

Firstly, home assignments maintain continuity, interest and energy, and therefore act as a 'bridge' between meetings. Secondly, home assigments give clients an opportunity to explore a topic in more depth and in their own time. Thirdly, undertaking home assignments implies that career counselling is not an event but a process, taking place over a period of time. During the contracting stage, clients will have understood that career counselling does not consist of a number of sessions which they passively 'attend', going away and forgetting about between meetings, but a process of thinking through and trying to make sense of past experience and present circumstances before considering the future. It involves self-analysis, making sense of the analysis, decision making and action, a process which clients will have begun before the first meeting and which will extend beyond their final meeting. The exercises and the counsellor are there to help, support and challenge clients during this period.

A fourth and related purpose is that home assignments put the client in the driving seat, as an active participant in the process. They build on the work of the contracting phase in obtaining and maintaining the client's involvement and ownership of the process. Home assignments imply that the client is the person who is responsible for doing the work; the counsellor is a facilitator to the person going through the career counselling process – a neutral assistant who can stand back and help the client to see and integrate patterns.

Finally, home assignments may point to themes and issues which are relevant to the client's career problem, either in the content itself or in the process. Home exercises are a sample of work, and there is useful information to be gleaned about the client from the way in which a task is approached. The manner in which clients present their exercises is often as revealing as the actual content, and can be a key to important counselling issues:

> Paul's home exercise consisted of six sheets of immaculately typed, very detailed work, enclosed in a neat folder. His counsellor almost gave him an A+ on the spot! A significant career issue for Paul was his perfectionism arising from need for approval.

> Stella came in for her session rather breathless and dishevelled, saying 'I didn't have much time to get those exercises done!' She scrabbled about in the bottom of an untidy briefcase to retrieve several dog-eared sheets covered in scrawled notes. Her chaotic approach to the exercise reflected the chaos of her life, both in and out of work.

Specific purposes

It may be appropriate to give clients an exercise for a specific purpose, relating to the point reached in the career counselling process as well as to meet individual client needs. If, for example, low self-esteem seems a block to career choice or career development, it might be helpful to give clients an exercise of writing down ten things they like about themselves, or some positive feedback they have received from others (see 'Self-validation exercise' on p. 58).

Who am I?

At this stage the counsellor's task is to assist clients in answering the question 'Who am I?'. As outlined in Chapter 3, they will have begun to do this already through their written preparation work and initial exploration at the first meeting.

Clients may need to develop self-understanding in the following areas:

- Skills (What can I do now?)
- Values (What is important to me?)
- Interests (What am I really drawn towards?)
- Career drivers (What are my wants and needs from a career?)
- 'Past positives' (What resources have I gained from moments of personal pride, and experiences of achievement, satisfaction, managing personal change or enjoyment?)
- Personal attributes (What strengths do I bring to my work? And what areas might I want to develop?)
- Aptitudes (What abilities or level am I capable of attaining?).

In asking clients for their initial self-assessment, it is important to encourage them to be specific. Clients will often make vague statements such as:

- I enjoy responsibility.
- I'm a creative person.
- I'm hopeless with numbers.
- I want to do something more worthwhile.
- I need a challenge.
- I'm good with people.
- I don't have enough variety in my job.

Concepts like 'creative' and 'worthwhile' can mean different things to different people. The meaning a word carries for the individual should be explored, and the client can be gently challenged if his or her own perception seems inaccurate.

Client (Cl):	I'm just not a creative person.
Career counsellor (Cc):	What do you mean by creative?
Cl:	Well, I'd love to paint and draw, even play a musical instrument. But I always felt it was a lost cause, as my brothers were so much more talented.
Cc:	So, being creative involves being as good as your brothers?
Cl:	Hmm … it did then.
Cc:	And now?
Cl:	I don't know. I guess I'm being a bit hard on myself.
Cc:	Supposing you were a little easier on yourself. What would you start saying?

The counsellor can formulate hunches about the way clients' skills, values, interests, personal qualities and aptitudes are being used (or not) in their work. Clients can be helped to assess themselves systematically through the use of written assignments and also through using psychometric tests and questionnaires. Later, the counsellor can check out how any questionnaire results match up with earlier hunches. Chapter 5 looks at the use of tests and questionnaires in career counselling.

Examples of exercises

The exercises described below are not meant to be prescriptive, but will be used to highlight certain principles and to show how home assignments can fit into the process of career counselling.

Enjoyable events exercise

Purpose: Many people tend to forget about their 'highs', or take them for granted. The purpose of this exercise is twofold. Firstly, to remind clients of positive experiences that may have been forgotten; this can be uplifting, particularly if clients see their current situation as rather gloomy. Secondly, it helps clients to identify any patterns of enjoyable events, such as 'the importance of working closely together with others', which may assist with career planning,

Method: The client is asked to list a number of enjoyable events and to identify what was enjoyable about them. The client is also asked to identify any qualities used, and to attempt to draw out important themes. For example, rock climbing may require physical fitness, organisation, cooperative team effort.

A depressed client may need encouragement from the counsellor to bring out these memories. It may help to suggest that a client 'thinks small' by saying: 'Your enjoyable event does not have to be a huge thing or something where you were judged by another person. It should be something *you* enjoyed.'

Sometimes patterns are very obvious to clients, and they will instantly describe the main themes. For other clients the themes really need to be drawn out through discussion. Sometimes the exercise creates a surprise:

> Jan had been working in a fairly solitary occupation as a researcher, and had always thought she was someone who preferred to work alone. She was surprised to find a strong theme of enjoying being with people and engaging in joint projects.

Some clients, in our experience, remark that 'None of my enjoyable events were in work.' Whilst this is of interest, it is important to prevent the client from concluding 'therefore I have never enjoyed my work'. An emphasis on the *patterns* underlying the events will go some way to prevent this from happening.

This exercise can put clients in touch with their real selves. When people are in a state of 'enjoying', they are likely to be intuitive, able to be truly themselves, and most free from the influence of their 'introjected values' (see pp. 67–9). From this position, clients are more likely to be able to identify in an instinctive way important themes and directions for the future. Clearly, responsibilities and practical circumstances have to be taken into account, and realistically most people do not earn a full-time living from doing something they enjoy all the time. It is likely that clients will have to compromise to some degree:

> Judy had been good at art at school, but was discouraged from pursuing it as a
> career by her parents and teachers and had gone into secretarial work. Her
> 'enjoyable events' came up with strong artistic themes, and as she discussed them
> she seemed to 'come alive'. At the age of 40, although she was very bored with
> secretarial work, as a single parent with a mortgage she was unable to take the risk
> of pursuing art as a full-time career. Following career counselling, however, she did
> several evening classes in painting, began to produce handmade greetings cards
> and gained a lot of satisfaction and enjoyment from selling them at a friend's market
> stall from time to time. She also did a couple of graphics packages with Learndirect,
> after which she was able to obtain more interesting secretarial assignments.

Satisfying achievements exercise

Purpose: As with the 'Enjoyable events' exercise, the purpose of this exercise is to
raise self-esteem by focusing on positive memories, and to identify patterns of
skills which clients may want to use in their career.

Method: The client is asked to list a number of satisfying achievements and to
pinpoint what was satisfying about them. It is important to stress what the client
personally finds satisfying, rather than achievements that pleased other people
(unless this coincides with the client being pleased as well). The client is then
asked to identify the skills and qualities used, and attempt to draw out important
themes. It may help the client, in thinking about the skills used, to refer to a list of
skills (see Nathan and Floyed, 2002).

For some clients, achievements are not necessarily to do with work:

> Paul's achievements were all leisure related (sporting success, winning prizes for
> gardening), although he said he felt these successes 'didn't count'. He saw himself
> as a bit of a 'wimp' at work, for being afraid to take risks. The counsellor pointed out
> that his potholing exploits had required great courage. Paul realised that he had
> been unable to take risks at work because of fear of failing his father. In the leisure
> sphere this didn't matter – the pressure only applied to work achievement.

The relationship between achievement and enjoyment

There is sometimes a dynamic between satisfying achievements and enjoyable
events. For example, all of the enjoyable events might describe holidays and other
'time-off' activities. This might show that a person is under stress, and holidays
are enjoyable because they provide a means of escape. If considered alone, this
exercise does not show that the person is active or interested in anything other
than getting away from the pressures. However, it may be useful to explore how
much importance a client places on achievement, responsibility and pressure in
work and leisure.

The 'Satisfying achievements' exercise is based on the assumption that career counselling is concerned with helping people to achieve more success and satisfaction in their work, and that there may be a connection between what people have succeeded at in the past and what they will want to do in the future. It is, however, not necessarily true that what has been satisfying in the past is either enjoyable or an indicator of what clients *want* to do in the future, as this case study demonstrates:

> Janet was a sensitive and artistic child. She was brilliant at maths and her parents encouraged her to study it at degree level. In her final year, her father suggested she took up actuarial work as a career, and expressed great pleasure when Janet made a success of this too. Ten years later, Janet described her work as 'bleak' and the world she worked in as 'grey and colourless'. Janet was given the 'Enjoyable events' and 'Satisfying achievements' exercises to do. It became clear that, although she found mathematical problems interesting, and gained intellectual *satisfaction* from problem solving, there was no sense of *enjoyment* for her in what she did. Her enjoyable events mostly involved people and participation in the arts. She was able to see that she had spent many years pleasing her father, and decided it was time to please herself – as she described it, to take a more 'colourful road'.

Transferable skills exercise

Purpose: To raise awareness of skills used and gained in the past and present; to gain clarity on areas of competence of greatest *interest*; to produce a list of the most transferable skills; to gain feedback from others on skills.

Method: A comprehensive list of skills is given to the client to self-assess. The client then chooses three or more co-raters.

Many people discount their skills unless they are linked to paid employment, usually their most recent job. Career counselling can help people to evaluate the skills they have gained from all parts of their lives, for example, through hobbies and interests, voluntary work and service to the community, and in being 'only a housewife and mother'. This can help people to gain the confidence to transfer such skills to an appropriate work environment.

Hopson and Scally (1991) present a useful classification of skills in four categories: skills with 'data' (for example, classifying data); 'ideas' (for example, expressing ideas orally); 'people' (for example, resolving conflict); and 'things' (for example, using machinery). Clients can assess the range of skills they have and rate their level of competence by using a skills inventory (see Nathan and Floyed, 2002). If the client gives a copy of the skills inventory form to someone else for an independent assessment, comparisons between the two sets of ratings can be revealing:

> Althea's sister rated her as more competent in the communication and negotiation skills area than she rated herself. After some discussion with her counsellor, Althea realised that she tended to take these skills for granted and undervalue them, probably because she had gained them within the context of being 'only' a housewife and mother, rather than through 'proper' work experience.

Sometimes it is valuable to encourage the client to get several people to rate their skills – people who have known them in different contexts.

> James asked five people to rate his skills. He was surprised that they generally saw him as more creative than he saw himself. This led to a discussion of James's schooling, where he had been told by an art teacher that he was not artistic. James thus realised that he *had* been using creative skills all along, which led him to feel more relaxed about his current situation.

If clients are working at a managerial or professional level, they might find a 360-degree feedback exercise of use. Often based on research into competencies or skills, such an exercise can provide a realistic and relatively objective picture of how a client's behaviours are rated by peers, direct reports, managers, friends and family. The choice of 'assessors' will clearly influence the results; clients should be made aware that the exercise will show how they relate to, and are seen by, this *particular* group. They need to choose people whose opinions they value, and who will not be destructive or overly admiring.

Approaches on offer vary. A computer-generated report on a range of competencies relevant to the client's level of responsibility can provide a useful focus in a development or coaching discussion (Pilat is an example of one of many companies supplying 360-degree feedback reports – see Appendix G).

Values exercise

Purpose: To review what is important in work and non-work, and what, if anything, has changed.
Method: Use a 'Values' exercise, such as suggested in Nathan and Floyed (2002).

Values in relation to work represent the degree to which a person regards his or her work as worthwhile. This 'worthwhileness' includes the amount of power, autonomy, creativity, learning, altruism, security, status and money which are sought in work.

In career counselling, it can sometimes assist clients to distinguish between their work and non-work values. For example, it may be very important for a person to express his or her creativity outside, but not necessarily in, work.

Values may not be stable in a person. A young man leaving school may decide to forgo the prospect of more academic work for the lure of his first car in a smart sales position. This gives him status among his peers, independence and money. Ten years later he finds himself out of a job, with no car and no qualifications. Or he cannot see himself getting any further with his present employer. Or, for whatever reason, money and status are no longer so attractive. As we outlined in Chapter 2, values can change at any time of life, but may particularly be affected by a major life event (for example, marriage, divorce, serious illness, redundancy, parenthood, religious conversion) or a more surreptitious transition, such as 'reaching 40'.

The following case demonstrates the way changes in personal values can be addressed in career counselling:

> Peter was 35 years old and married with two children. With a successful career in sales and marketing, he had all the 'trappings' of success. But he felt restless. He was unhappy with the increasing necessity to play the 'political game' in order to advance his career. It emerged in the first meeting that he was disappointed with the way 'society had turned out'. His early faith in people had been shattered by the pushing and shoving he observed, received and was expected to give, just in order to 'get on'. He was angry that he was being challenged to drop his childhood values that 'people should help each other'.

Career counselling helped Peter address the real importance to him of these altruistic values. A good deal of confusion was highlighted in the discussions, and Peter eventually decided on a compromise which allowed for a more even balance between the 'altruistic' and 'power' values in his life.

Self-validation exercise

Purpose: To raise self-esteem and develop a more positive self-image which can be related to future options. Clients with low self-esteem tend to focus on their bad points. This exercise asks clients to list their positive attributes – things they like about themselves but which are not usually in the foreground of their awareness because they tend to be taken for granted or simply never thought about.

Method 1:   Suggest categories of qualities, such as 'physical', 'mental' and 'social', or ask clients to think of situations when they feel good about themselves. Examples of qualities include strength, appearance, coordination (physical), problem-solving and creative abilities (mental), friendliness and warmth (social).

Method 2:   Another way of encouraging clients to bring out the qualities they like in themselves is to ask them to complete, say, ten sentences, beginning with 'I feel good about myself when …'

> Roland was initially stumped when asked to identify ten things he liked or valued in himself. However, with gentle but firm encouragement from his career counsellor, he realised that he appreciated his dress sense, his tennis-playing ability, his sensitivity to the plight of stray animals and his knowledge of malt whiskies! This positive discussion about himself led Roland to value more openly some aspects of himself which he had tended to discount. He also realised that he needed to be doing work with a higher physical component.

Summarising the self-information gathered

During this stage of the career counselling process, through discussion of home assignments and through the process of completing tests and questionnaires (see

---

Box 4.1 Summary chart example

SKILLS
- List your top eight transferable skills
- Skills to develop?
- Use less of?

SATISFYING ACHIEVEMENTS
- Key themes

PERSONAL QUALITIES
- Up to ten strengths

INTERESTS
- Top six (see Chapter 5, p. 77) themes

WORK VALUES
- Top eight, bottom four

ENJOYABLE EVENTS
- Key themes

REFLECTIONS
- What does all this say about me?
- Common themes?
- Discrepancies?
- Initial ideas?

Chapter 5) and receiving feedback, clients will be accumulating a wealth of information about themselves, and so will gain a more confident self-understanding. This forms a springboard for thinking about options for the future. For example, a client may be developing a self-perception, 'I am a very outgoing person', which helps to encourage the attitude: 'and so the implications are that in order to gain job satisfaction, I should now consider doing ...' (things that conform to this more confident self-understanding).

An excellent way to synthesise and summarise the self-assessment information accumulated is to ask the client to produce a summary chart – see Box 4.1.

Ask clients to produce their summary sheet on A1 (flipchart size) paper, using coloured pens. This faciliates an overall view of any common themes and/or discrepancies, and makes it easier to talk through with the career counsellor at the next meeting (or to share with co-partcipants in a workshop setting). Later, clients might also like to produce an A4 version for ease of reference.

Jamie found his summary chart very useful: he realised that he was consistently showing a strong need for 'challenge' – which is what was missing in his job. Yet he also realised that his strong family values, and his need for a good work–life balance, were influencing his decision making.

The summary chart then provides a natural focus for producing a list of 'job satisfiers' (see p. 63 and p. 168).

What do I want?

During the first meeting it may be appropriate to elicit from clients any options they are considering for the future. However, a client will need an awareness of his or her occupational self before attempting to answer this question.

One way to elicit occupational ideas would be to suggest that clients look through a website or directory of occupational information (see Appendix C and Chapter 5). In many cases, however, it may be more fruitful to bring out into the open any fantasies clients may have about their future, or unfulfilled passions left over from childhood or adolescence. Such fantasies can deter the person from acting rationally. Box 4.2 lists some suggestions for doing this.

Box 4.2 Suggestions for eliciting occupational fantasies

- If you had a year off, how would you spend it?
- What are the three things you feel most passionate about (dream about, think about, read about, talk about, would do voluntarily)?
- If you could be anything/anyone you wanted, what/who would you like to be?
- Without thinking much about it, finish off the sentence 'I want to …'. (This can be done several times.)
- What were your early dreams about what you might do or be when you grew up? (If the client says 'I don't know' or 'I didn't have any', follow up gently with 'What might they have been?')
- Describe an ideal day. (Helpful questions: 'What are you doing?' 'What do you see?' 'What does it feel like?')

One or more of the suggestions in Box 4.2 can be tackled either during the counselling meeting or as a home assignment. (See also the 'Guided fantasy' exercise on pp. 100–1, which can be used *once* a client has alighted on a particular idea. Such an exercise can help to make it more real, and thus motivate the client to explore it further.)

Describing a 'preferred future': the solution-focused approach

The solution-focused approach is of great relevance to career counselling. A good time to introduce this approach is at the 'What do I want?' stage, when clients need a framework for constructing a view of their preferred future. Box 4.3 describes the qualities of a well-defined preferred future.

Box 4.3 The qualities of a well-defined preferred future

- Positive: what is wanted, rather than what is not wanted
- Small, concrete and observable
- Significant to the client
- Realistic
- Recognised as involving hard work
- Beginnings rather than endings

The miracle question

The miracle question is a useful and creative way of helping clients to articulate their hopes for the future. Note that the miracle question has four parts:

1 That a miracle happens.
2 The miracle realises the goal.
3 The client is 'asleep' (so doesn't know it is happening).
4 The discovery – step-by-step.

The exercise below makes use of the 'Job satisfiers' exercise (see p. 63 and p. 168).

Imagine you have gone home to sleep and you wake up the next morning and realise that a miracle has happened and all your job satisfiers are being completely met, and you feel a huge sense of satisfaction …

Prompt questions:

- How will you know that this miracle has happened? What first steps will tell you?
- What will you be doing differently? … What else?
- How will you be feeling?
- What will you be doing differently to show others you are feeling this?
- What will others (for example, family, friends) be noticing?
- What will your clients/customers be doing as a result of noticing that the miracle has happened?
- What will your colleagues be doing to show you they have noticed?
- What's the most significant thing that you are doing differently to indicate to you and to others that the miracle has occurred?

Once the client has described the miracle, the 'scaling' technique can be used to enable clients to evaluate how far advanced they are towards the 'miracle', and to set goals. See Chapter 6, p. 99 for continued discussion of applying scaling to action planning. Scaling uses the following principles:

- describes small steps to progress;
- builds on success and resources;
- 'if it works, keep doing it'; and
- provides a quantitative way to measure success.

Questions to evaluate where clients are now and where they could realistically get to

Ask clients to review the job satisfiers in the light of their current roles and the future. Use the following prompts:

- Where are you now in terms of your role meeting your job satisfiers, 10 being the 'miracle scenario', 0 being the 'worst case'?
- What tells you that?
- What makes the score 'x' and not 0?
- What is it that you are doing that makes your score 'x' and not 0?
- Where on the scale represents good enough for you, the point where you would settle?

- How will you know that you are there?
- What particular job satisfier/s would have to be more fully accomplished to meet your desire for change?
- What key resources do you bring to make the desired change/s?
- How would you know if you were using them effectively?

Jan (see p. 63) described her 'miracle' as having a role where she could influence policy as well as contribute to research, where the organisation and her boss would value and recognise her contribution. She described her 'future self' as someone who would 'walk tall' in the eyes of others, and offer constructive suggestions much more than at present. When asked to say where she was now on a scale of 1 to 10, she said '5'. 'How come you are a '5', and not a zero?', her career counsellor asked? Jan answered that there were odd times when she did feel valued and could contribute, but this happened all too infrequently. When asked to describe a point on the scale that would be represent good enough progress, Jan said '7'. A '7', she said, would be seeking recognition from people other than her boss: her colleagues and even her boss's boss. It would also mean that she would make sure people knew about what she was achieving and doing well.

As a result, Jan became much more active in promoting her achievements, which helped tide her over a difficult time. It also helped her enormously in preparing for and conducting her job search.

A useful reference is Greene and Grant (2003). For further training in the UK , contact the Brief Therapy Practice (see Appendix G).

It is important at this stage to strike a balance between encouraging clients to use their imagination and ignoring the constraints of the real world, and not brushing aside the outer objective realities of the client's life, and failing to demonstrate an understanding of the very real, practical limitations clients may face. Most career decisions are a compromise, as the following case study demonstrates:

Alistair was a highly paid but frustrated and unhappy solicitor specialising in company law. He had a strong interest in helping young people, and had considered retraining as a probation officer. However, with four school-age children and elderly parents to support, it was unrealistic to change direction completely. He eventually found some compromise outlets for the 'caring' side of his nature by moving to a job within the legal profession which involved training young solicitors, and by working at a local youth club one night a week.

Realism in decision making may subsequently be increased by relating enhanced self-awareness to accurate occupational information. An exercise ('Satisfiers vs. options') which can be used to help the client at this stage will be found in Chapter 6.

Some clients will need longer to reach the point where they are sufficiently in touch with their own desires and potential to answer the question 'What do I want?' constructively. There may also be times when, even with increased self-understanding and an idea of where they want to be, clients will feel 'stuck' when they try to think about getting what they want. The 'Job satisfiers' exercise is a useful way of translating the themes from the summary sheet into a work-related format.

Job satisfiers exercise

Purpose: For clients who are at the stage of having accumulated information about themselves from homework assignments and tests, this exercise helps them to synthesise and summarise the information into a 'job template'.

Method: Clients are asked to consider their work preferences and other factors which are necessary for their job satisfaction, by reviewing the data they have gathered about themselves from all sources and listing the specific elements they want in their next job. The following case study illustrates the outcome of such an exercise.

Jan's post as a researcher with a public service organisation was 'deleted' at a time when she was looking around for another job, as she was so dissatisfied at work. She wanted to be able to understand the reasons for her frustration, as well as establishing a career direction for the future. By the final meeting, with some help from the career counsellor, she had synthesised all the self-understanding information she had, and produced the list of 'Job satisfiers' in Box 4.4.

Box 4.4 Jan's 'Job satisfiers' exercise

- Work providing intellectual stimulation
- Work making use of analytical skills
- Work making use of oral/written communication skills
- Work making use of organisational skills
- Solving complex problems
- Collaboration with colleagues
- Freedom to set own schedule and work at own pace
- A clear role responding to a felt need in the organisation
- Work which has an impact on decision making
- Work where high standards are valued
- A visible, central role (not 'backroom')
- An innovative, progressive environment

Clearly, such a list as that in Box 4.4 represents something of an ideal, almost impossible to obtain in full measure in any career. However, it is a useful list which can form a basis for evaluating the suitability of various future options for a client (see Satisfiers vs. options exercise in Chapter 6).

Clients will often benefit from clarifying their job satisfiers, which need to be specific enough to use in a job search. Thus, 'I want to work with people' is far too general; 'I want the main part of my work to be rehabilitating learning disabled youngsters' is much more specific and useful. Check also that no job satisfier is omitted, by referring to the client's summary sheet (see p. 59).

Integrating the exercises into the counselling

It is important to allow sufficient time between meetings for clients to complete their assignments. In the gaps between sessions, clients can also discuss their thoughts with a partner, friend or other significant person.

As well as addressing the content of the home assignments ('What did you learn or gain from it?'), clients can be asked how they felt about doing an exercise (see also Chapter 5, pp. 80–1). For some clients, an exercise may involve confronting aspects of themselves or their past which may be difficult or painful to face. If painful feelings have been raised, this may need to be explored in the next meeting. In some cases, clients may make an attempt to do an exercise but be unable to complete it. Not all clients will wish to delve into the issues that are blocking them, and it may be possible in any case to make a 'good enough' career decision without opening up painful areas (see Chapter 8).

When a client has decided to take psychometric tests (see Chapter 5), it is helpful to begin the feedback session with some discussion of the outcome of any home assignments. Such a discussion can set the scene: the themes that emerge from the exercises can then be related to themes arising from the test feedback. For example, in the case of Jan, her strong need to work closely with others emerged as a theme from the 'Enjoyable events' exercise and was echoed later in results from personality and occupational interest questionnaires (see also Chapter 5, pp. 76–7).

What resources can help me move on?
What is stopping me?

By now, the career counselling will have enabled the clients to gather some 'self-information', which they have summarised and translated into a list of specific job satisfiers. At this stage, some kind of ideas generation or brainstorming exercise will be useful; see p. 100 for a description of a 'Guided fantasy' exercise. An exercise to enable the client to produce job ideas can be found in Nathan and Floyed (2002).

The job of the career counsellor is to assist the client to make an initial assessment of the viability of the option, and of any further research needing to be undertaken. This can help the client to avoid wasting valuable time researching an unrealistic idea, or being put off a possibility without due evidence.

Blocks and bridges exercise

Purpose: To identify a client's external and internal resources, both present and lacking, in relation to a job idea.

Method: Ask the client to write down a list of 'bridges' – the resources he or she has which would help to achieve the job idea. Typical bridges include skills, training, qualifications, experience, support from others, motivation, personal qualities, contacts, knowledge, health, money, the job market (now and in the future). Blocks may include a lack of the necessary bridges, family responsibilities, another person who might stand in the way and any 'self-limiting beliefs', including fear of change (see p. 100).

Once the client has completed the list, talk them through it, with the summary chart (see p. 59) in view. Check how realistic they are and identify ways in which some of the blocks could be overcome. Help the client to identify any bridges left out, and whether applying some of the bridges could overcome a key block.

Kieran's brainstorm produced 'occupational psychology' as a very attractive option. These were Kieran's key blocks and bridges:

Bridges:

- 20 years' experience in industry and human resource management
- Strong analytical skills
- Enough money to live for two years
- Support of wife
- Great attraction to subject
- Contacts in human resources

Blocks:

- No first degree, and no recent experience of study
- My age – job market for 45+
- Studying with people half my age
- Fear of failure
- Lack of contacts in occupational psychology

Initial discussion led Kieran to realise that he was greatly attracted to the subject and felt he had a good deal to contribute from his experience. But he did not know enough about the kind of jobs available and whether his age would be a barrier. This needed to be checked out further, through talking to people working in the field. Most important, however, was Kieran's lack of belief in his ability to 'make it' in a new area that relied on strong academic attainment.

When faced with an 'internal' block, it is useful for career counsellors to be equipped with some approaches to help clients address this.

At this stage optimism and positive feelings about the future are often held in check by pessimism and negative emotions, with the net result that the client feels 'stuck'. In most blocked career situations, both external and internal constraints exist, as Carla's case demonstrates:

Carla had already applied for six marketing jobs without success when she came for career counselling.

Carla:	Marketing is just too competitive to get into.
Career counsellor (Cc):	It must be very down-heartening to have to battle away in the face of these job rejections.

(Continued)

(Continued)

Carla: [*silence*] ... Oh dear, I just can't see myself getting anywhere – I really wanted to get a marketing role – maybe I'm just not good enough – there are obviously so many good people out there.

Cc: [*perceiving the possibility of a significant internal block*] Yes, it is competitive. And you want this role?

Carla: Yes, but I'm clearly not getting anywhere. It's pretty hopeless.

Cc: So, what tells you that you're not good enough?

Carla: I'm getting rejected for every job I go for.

Cc: What was the furthest you got?

Carla: Well, I got to two final interviews.

Cc: So near ...

Carla: And so far.

Cc: Did you get any feedback?

Carla: I did from one of them – I always used to ask for feedback, but I'm fed up now; they just say anything plausible.

Cc: What did this one tell you?

Carla: Actually, they said it was a close run thing. In the end, the other person could start earlier than I could – they were pretty impressed with what I'd done.

Cc: In particular?

Carla: Oh, my new business work and so on.

Cc: What did you actually achieve?

Although career counselling could not change the job situation, it helped to unravel the feelings and thoughts that were getting in the way of Carla acting with as much assertion and determination as she could to approach the job market. Counselling also helped Carla to work on her feelings of not being good enough. She constantly put herself down; her counsellor pointed this out, and gradually Carla was able to interrupt her put-downs herself. She was given an exercise to write a list of her accomplishments in life, including the difficulties she had overcome. As the counselling progressed, she began to say to herself: 'Although it may take some time to get the job I want because entry is competitive, I'm as good as anyone else. I need to make a lot more applications using a variety of methods.'

Like Carla, many clients have a tendency to see constraints as external, and need help to recognise that there are internal blocks too, for example, low self-esteem, high levels of anxiety, guilt about the effects of a decision on significant others, anger and frustration about the existing situation, or ambivalence. Such a recognition can enable clients to develop new and more productive perspectives for the future. In this section we examine some of the sorts of 'roadblocks' which may be in the way of clients achieving their goals, and how clients can be helped to unravel, understand and deal with various constraints.

Emotional triggering

Career counsellors need to be alert to instances where a client describes an experience which is similar in some respect to an event in the past. The recent event

Figure 4.1   Emotional triggering (Carla's example)

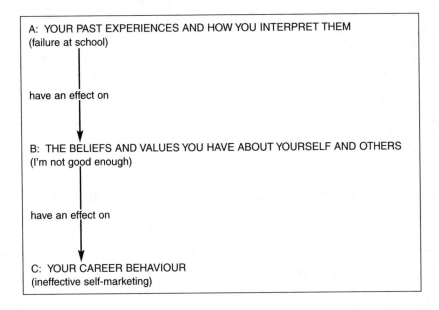

may act as an emotional trigger, causing the level and type of emotion associated with the early painful event to be re-experienced. For example, enabling Carla to move on involved making the connection between her current feelings, 'I'm not good enough', and past experiences of failure at school, as Figure 4.1 demonstrates.

Career counselling often needs to address 'A' and 'B' in order to change 'C'. Cathartic interventions are particularly appropriate in enabling the client to release painful emotion attached to past experiences when emotional triggering occurs. Some of the origins of irrational beliefs and values are now examined.

Introjected values

Introjection is a central concept in Gestalt therapy (see Clarkson, 2004). Introjected values are unquestioned (usually unconscious) values which are based on the messages clients have received from other people (often their parents) earlier in life. When people 'swallow whole' ideas of what they believe others want them to be, life becomes acting a part. The underlying message with introjected values is 'You're only OK if ...' (if you obey the 'shoulds'/'should nots'). Introjected values can therefore prevent people from accurately perceiving themselves and the world, which may lead to faulty career decisions. For further discussion of this extreme form of self-doubt, see Clarkson (2003).

The following case study is of a man who lost touch with his 'real self' because he learned to please his parents by becoming the sort of little boy that his parents required, in order to be loved:

John had obtained a degree in mechanical engineering, although he found it a struggle and only achieved a third. He hated the industrial placement he had undergone as part of his studies, and did not want to pursue engineering as a career. In an emotional session, it emerged that John was given a Meccano set when he was little, and always had lots of praise and attention from his father when he did practical things. The session was cathartic, and John began to realise that he would probably survive, even if his father withdrew his love. He had a warm personality and a strong interest in helping people, and decided to investigate retraining as a massage therapist.

Some examples of introjected values which frequently emerge in career counselling are listed in Box 4.5.

Box 4.5 Introjected values

You should:

- get a secure job
- be a career woman
- be perfect
- be more successful than your parents
- make upward progress within a hierarchy
- have a respectable professional job
- go to university
- get into a well-known company
- make up your mind what to do and stick to it for the rest of your working life
- get married and be a good mother
- make a lot of money

You should not:

- take risks
- go into a traditionally 'male' job (for a woman)
- go into a traditionally 'female' job (for a man)
- change direction
- be more/less successful than your parents
- waste your qualifications
- take a drop in salary

Many clients are not aware of their introjected values, and do not consciously state them. The career counsellor should listen very carefully for themes which indicate that an introjected value is operating, as the case studies of Paul and Stella indicate:

Paul had started a graduate training scheme with a bank, ostensibly because his friends were all going to work in the City. However, he was never really happy from day one. After a year, he was finding it impossible to pursue alternatives, because every time he began to look at the jobs pages in the paper, he felt terrible pangs of guilt. His father had recently retired after working as an accountant for 40 years.

Paul's strong introjected values were 'Make up your mind what to do and stick to it for the rest of your working life', together with 'Don't take risks – get a nice steady, secure nine-to-five job.'

Stella was 40. With a recent divorce and two teenage children, she felt at a loss about what to do. In one career counselling session, her counsellor pointed out that she had spent more time talking about her children's career choices and her ex-husband's career difficulties than her own career future.

Stella's introjected values told her 'Get married and be a good mother' and 'Devote yourself to others.'

The counsellor's job is to help people see how their situation has come about, to get them to question whether their introjected values are doing them a service or a disservice, and to facilitate the release of emotion. Often it will be sufficient to reflect back the theme to the client. Counselling can also encourage the client to distinguish between their 'shoulds' and their 'wants' by gently challenging the introjected values:

John:	I did all that training – it seems a waste.
Career counsellor (Cc):	A waste of your qualifications?
John:	Yes – I should make use of them.
Cc:	Who says?
John:	My father – he keeps telling me I should stick with engineering.
Cc:	What would happen if you did?
John:	I'd become more and more unhappy.
Cc:	It seems that your father has given you some strong messages about what you *should* do. Let's look at what you *want* to do.

For clients who have lived their whole life by 'shoulds', identifying their 'wants' may be a long-term project, and referral for personal counselling may be required.

Self-limiting beliefs

Whereas introjected values are largely unconscious and are unlikely to be directly expressed by clients, self-limiting beliefs are statements which the client will actually make (see Box 4.6).

Box 4.6 Self-limiting beliefs

- I don't need anyone's help.
- 'X' will sort it all out for me.
- I can't live on less than I earn now.
- It's undignified to have to promote yourself.
- Somewhere there's the perfect job.
- There's no point planning ahead when there's so much change afoot.
- Nobody will take me seriously.
- Life is so unfair to me.
- Everyone else is better off than me.
- I won't be good enough.
- It's safer not to try than to risk failure.
- If I do well enough, Mum/Dad will love me.
- I'll fail.
- It's so competitive, I'd never get in.
- Everything will be OK when I get a new job.
- I can't change anything – I don't have any power.
- It's too late.
- If I wait long enough, things will change.
- I'm too old/young/overqualified/underqualified.
- I can't help the way I am – it's just the way I'm made.

Career counsellors can help clients to identify, challenge and change such beliefs, for example:

Client:	I won't be good enough.
Career counsellor:	What *would* be good enough?
	Good enough *in whose eyes?*
	Good enough *for what?*
[or more challenging]	Is this what you want?

Each challenging response by the counsellor encourages the client to look more specifically at the 'I won't be good enough' statement. 'What would be?' demands a positive response. 'In whose eyes?' forces the client to identify whether there is a 'judge' left over from previous experiences. 'For what?' stimulates the client to relate the 'I won't be good enough' statement to specific criteria.

The effect of challenging interventions can be that the client is able to reassess the validity of the self-limiting belief, and develop a readiness to respond to opportunities in a more rational way.

Making the best use of home assignments

- Always ask clients how they found any home assignment.
- Don't assume, because a client has not written down their responses to an exercise, that he or she has not thought about the topic. For some clients, writing down such thoughts may be difficult, implying a commitment they are not yet ready to make.

- Ensure that you talk through the assignment with the client, perhaps focusing on one or two areas in some detail (for example, in 'Enjoyable events' or 'Satisfying achievements') as well as considering overall themes.
- Assure the client that all exercises will be addressed, even if it is later on following the completion of the summary chart and 'Job satisfiers' exercise.
- When giving clients instructions for completing the exercises, go through the instructions and address any uncertainties, including the client's time availability. Reassure clients that some other clients, too, have found these exercises a 'bit of a struggle' at first (you want clients to feel all right, even if they do struggle with an exercise), especially a 'blank sheet' exercise such as 'Satisfying achievements'. If appropriate, reduce the number of achievements you ask the client to provide.

We hope that these few exercises give a flavour of how home assignments can be used in career counselling. A summary of some key exercises can be found in Appendix H. Trained career counsellors will find a larger selection of exercises in Nathan and Floyed (2002).

Summary

In this chapter we have described the process of enabling clients to develop a comprehensive and objective understanding of the assets they have in relation to the world of work, to develop some ideas about future goals and gain insight into ways in which they may be blocking themselves from moving on. The career counsellor needs to be particularly alert to themes about job satisfaction (what the client finds satisfying and rewarding), and themes about blocks to action (how the person is stopping him/herself from moving on). Cathartic and challenging skills are also very important at this stage. Giving home assignments to clients should *always* be combined with sufficient time to discuss and explore the exercises.

In Chapter 5 we discuss in more detail the use of tests and questionnaires. We show how feedback can assist clients' awareness of their strengths and weaknesses in relation to the world of work. The chapter concludes with an examination of occupational information and its uses within a career counselling framework.

Checklist: Enabling clients' understanding

☑ Use good basic counselling skills throughout the career counselling.
☑ Help clients to identify themes emerging from the exercises.
☑ Use 'home assignments' as a way of enriching the career counselling, and maintaining clients' commitment between meetings.
☑ Use home assignments and any other exercises to enable clients to make clear and specific statements about themselves.
☑ Use a 'summary chart' to bring all the information together.
☑ Encourage clients to identify fantasy jobs and environments, but follow this with a consideration of realistic constraints, external and internal.
☑ Be alert to 'irrational' constraints driven by strong 'I should or 'I should not' statements, or self-limiting beliefs.

5 Using Tests, Questionnaires and Occupational Information

This chapter is divided into two sections. We will begin by looking at ways in which the timely and sensitive use of psychometric tests and other questionnaires (covering, for example, aptitudes, occupational interests, career 'drivers' and personality) can significantly assist the process of career counselling. The counsellor and client can still operate in a collaborative mode, using tests and other assessment exercises as resources to stimulate discussion and to develop the client's own self-understanding. Initial contracting will have ensured, as far as possible, that clients understand this use of questionnaires.

In the second section we examine the role that occupational information can play. We believe that career counsellors should not be expert providers of occupational information to clients, but that they do need to know of sufficient resources to support clients in their research. We will present some guidelines for making use of occupational information in ways consistent with a career counselling framework.

Using tests and questionnaires in career counselling

The benefits of using tests in career counselling
There *are* ways in which timely and sensitive use of psychometric and other questionnaires can significantly assist the process of career counselling. Such an approach can:

- provide a framework for dialogue;
- increase clarity and confidence;
- provoke new personal insights;
- assist long-term perspectives;
- reduce the risk of haphazard decision making; and
- help to explain past behaviour at work.

Provide a framework for dialogue
The power of the printed word can be put to good use in career counselling. The fact that clients are asked to rate themselves on a scale of 1 to 10 for 'reserved – outgoing' can produce a rich discussion more easily than, to put it bluntly, the counsellor saying 'I would like to discuss with you how reserved or outgoing you are.'

The dialogue is further enhanced if clients are asked to make their own self-assessment first. It is through this self-assessment that clients are encouraged to take responsibility, thereby avoiding casting the counsellor in the role of judge.

Increase clarity and confidence

By being able to check self-perceptions on a variety of personal qualities, clients can come to be able to make quite confident statements about themselves. Discussion of test results, followed by further reflection and a subsequent counselling meeting, can lead to a confirmation of the client's self-view as well as acceptance of any surprises that emerge.

Provoke new personal insights

Some test results may enable clients to see themselves or the possibilities in a new light:

> Kathy (see p. 145 and p. 48) never fully appreciated her verbal capabilities. Aptitude tests showed a marked verbal superiority over her other aptitudes and the general population. Since she had not done well in her accountancy degree, this result and the ensuing counselling encouraged Kathy to trust this ability more. She began to consider careers where she might use her verbal abilities.

Assist long-term perspectives

When a client comes to accept an aspect of him- or herself, plans can be made for the future with the expectation that this characteristic will still be there in years to come. Alternatively, a clearer self-view following the use of tests can give a sense of control over the future which did not exist before.

Reduce the risk of haphazard decision making

The structure provided by the systematic and comprehensive array of tests and questionnaires can help clients to put their thoughts in order, and reduce the tendency to make decisions in a state of panic.

Help to explain past behaviour at work

'That explains it' is not an uncommon remark from clients who begin to see patterns emerging from test results and other exercises used in career counselling. For example, it may be that aptitude tests have shown that a person thinks quickly, but finds expressing thoughts in words is more difficult. Or a theme may emerge showing a preference for working with others rather than alone. This can explain why a person has been unhappy with a solitary occupation or self-employment.

How and when to introduce tests into the career counselling process

To enable tests to be seen by clients as an integral part of the career counselling process, they should be introduced alongside other self-assessment and home assignments, as resources which can provide evidence of patterns or themes of significance to the client. In the context of a collaborative counsellor–client relationship, they can be seen as just one more source of information.

Initial contracting can ensure that clients know about the fallibility of tests and that there is no question of 'pass or fail'. If clients are to be involved in a discussion of their expected results (prior to being given the actual scores), this can be mentioned as well. A written guidelines sheet can be given out explaining what to expect at the test session (see Appendix A).

Tests should not be given to clients before the first meeting. A meeting can provide a basis for deciding whether tests are likely to be of use for this client at this time. Occasionally, a client's degree of anxiety about his or her test performance will be so strong that counselling without testing, especially aptitude testing, might be more appropriate. This can be judged more accurately by a face-to-face meeting than by simply reading a client's written preparation.

Types of test and questionnaire used in career counselling

Although several different types of tests and questionnaires will be detailed here, we do not propose a lengthy description. The British Psychological Society has produced a comprehensive review of tests which are in common use for career development purposes. (See www.psychtesting.org.uk and click on the 'tests' section of the site. The site enables you to search the database of BPS-recognised tests for those most useful for 'counselling, advice, guidance and career change' applications (Newland Park Associates, 1991).

Aptitude tests

These tests have normative data, that is, they have been tested on a random or representative population. That population should be a valid comparison group for the individual undertaking the test. For example, one test we use has a 'general population' comparison group, as well as one for 'managerial and professional levels'. If using tests with a younger person, it may be appropriate to use a comparison group akin to the individual's educational attainment. From our experience in career counselling, the 'general population' group usually suffices when using a differential aptitude test (see below), as it allows the individual's natural capacities to be indicated, via the *difference*, not only the *level*, attained. A person's performance on the test is compared with that of others, and a 'profile' produced of relative strengths and weaknesses. Typical areas measured include abstract, verbal and numerical reasoning.

Such tests must be:

- *valid* – a test must measure what it purports to measure. The main types of validity include:

    - *content validity*, which relates to how well a test and behaviour are linked. If a test says it measures aptitude, then it should not include questions measuring attainment;
    - *construct validity*, which is the degree to which the test measures a theoretical construct such as verbal ability; and
    - *predictive validity*, which considers the degree to which a test can be seen to predict the quality measured; and

- *reliable* – it should provide a reasonably consistent indication of ability over time. Thus, if a group of people takes the same test twice, after a reasonable time has elapsed, and the results are identical, or almost identical, the test is likely to be reliable.

Every test should be accompanied by a manual, describing any research undertaken and giving figures for reliability and validity, and details of the population(s) on which it has been standardised. The technical aspects of test construction are well covered by Anastasi (1988).

A differential aptitude test can help to address the following kinds of question:

- Does the client learn better 'on the job' or through more academic means?
- Does the client have a stronger potential for working with figures or words?
- How quickly can the client think on his or her feet?
- Is the client more able to solve problems by grasping the 'whole' or by exploring the details?

Clients often ask for help in assessing their talents, capabilities and potential. In the following case, Denis was considering higher education:

> Denis had experienced no success, either at school or in work. His childhood had been strong on rejection and short on love. He had reacted by failing every exam, becoming violent, and indulging in excessive drinking, drug-taking and promiscuity. A trip from his native Zimbabwe to England resulted in a desire for a fresh start, following some pressure from his new English girlfriend. Denis had little idea of his aptitudes, as he had virtually no experience of testing them out.

Although success in higher education is dependent on many factors other than aptitude, it was appropriate to give Denis a relatively objective measure of his capabilities, which could be considered along with his interests, personal attributes and values. It emerged from the testing that his aptitudes were more suited to a practical, rather than academic, training. Counselling then focused on his dilemma of dealing with his girlfriend's pressure, as well as using his real aptitudes and interests.

Interests and motivation

Some questionnaires available are 'normative', that is, the client's 'scores' are compared with a general or particular population. For example, an individual's responses may indicate a greater liking for contact with people than the majority of the population. Other questionnaires may provide scales of particular characteristics as a way of systematically presenting the client's disparate answers to many questions (for example, Holland, 1983).

Where a client's interests are concerned, we prefer a different approach. Interests – that is, activities which are enjoyable and rewarding – are a vital key to what motivates a person. Ability alone is of little use without adequate interest to back it up. Unless people can understand and articulate their real interests, they may find themselves pushed in the direction that others want. As the following case shows, interests can become buried in the pursuit of pleasing others:

> Jenny had originally trained in teaching as it was 'what was expected of me' by family and teachers. 'I didn't want to be a nurse or secretary, and teaching was the only option left.' She did reasonably well at her job, but was quite content to give it up when she married John. After bringing up two children, Jenny approached a career counsellor about her lack of direction. Although she had maintained an interest in art and antiques since schooldays, she had never really considered seriously the possibility of art or antiques as a career option. Career counselling enabled Jenny to accept the legitimacy of pursuing her real interests.

The career counsellor can help clients to assess their interests by using some of the questions in Box 5.1.

Box 5.1 Self-assessment of interests

- What subjects did you like best at school?
- Which jobs/aspects of jobs have you enjoyed the most?
- What extra-mural classes have you attended with pleasure?
- What hobbies, interests and activities do you enjoy in your spare time?
- Which of these activities would be the last you would give up?
- What do you like to read about?
- Which skills do you most *like* using?
- Where do you spend your time?
- How do you spend your thinking time?

> By focusing on what he had enjoyed in the past, Ed gained the courage to pursue his long-held passion in a career. Ed had always loved working with his hands and creating something that looked good. In fact, he had originally trained to be a hairdresser. He also loved some time for solitude. But, with no academic qualifications, he took over his father's hairdressing business. In time, he became rather good at running and growing the business, and taking on new businesses. But his heart was never in it. Ten years later, it took a business failure for him to realise that he was getting little else from the work other than the thrill of developing a new business. He decided to re-train as an interior designer.

An occupational interests questionnaire may be based on Holland's six categories (Holland, 1983). Holland defined six types of people – Realistic, Intellectual,

Social, Conventional, Enterprising and Artistic – and six corresponding types of work environment. According to his theory, people seek out or create work environments which allow them to express their personalities and values. For example, people of the Enterprising orientation prefer to seek out environments which provide opportunities for persuading, dominating or leading others.

We have found that clients do not gain a great deal from receiving a 'score' on the Holland, or any other, categories. Rather, we conduct an in-depth discussion on what has attracted the client to particular activities highlighted in the questionnaire. This leads to the identification of themes, which the career counsellor must ensure are accurate and resonate with the client. This approach respects individual differences and avoids pigeonholing the client in one of a few categories.

> Johanna, George and Leila completed an interests questionnaire. One of the activities they all highlighted was 'to help developing countries to grow food'. Johanna was attracted to this activity as she would love to travel and to mix with people from different cultures. George, on the other hand, wanted to improve the lives of people less privileged. Leila had yet another reason: she was interested in the science and business of growing food more economically.

Personality

Human beings are very adaptable and square pegs can often force themselves into round holes, at least in the short term. Aspects of personality can facilitate a person's performance and achievement in certain careers, but limit success in others, as the case study of Clifford (the introverted sales representative, see pp. 28 and 30) illustrated.

> In the feedback discussion, Clifford's view of himself was challenged when a personality questionnaire suggested that he was quite reserved and shy. Counselling established that he had come to see himself as outgoing in order to believe that he could be successful in sales. He had also felt very competitive with a more outgoing younger brother, who had also been his father's favourite. These discoveries gave Clifford the confidence to let go of his desire to succeed in customer contact jobs, and to seek work more in sales administration.

Many people have little more than a vague idea of the personal attributes needed for success in different stages of career development. The process of career counselling can often bring about greater clarity and self-understanding through relatively objective and supportive feedback. The following case illustrates how interpersonal and 'political' skills are often considered to be part and parcel of success:

> Jim was referred for career counselling by his employer. He had been with the same employer for 20 years, but things had turned somewhat sour recently; he had fallen out with his boss, and felt very bruised by his recent appraisal. He wanted an opportunity to assess himself in an independent setting.

When Jim entered employment, he had no idea that, in order to 'get on', he would have to do more than simply perform his job tasks to the best of his ability. It came as a shock that he was also judged on how well he fitted in, particularly as far as his immediate boss was concerned. Career counselling enabled Jim to decide, with some relief, that he did not want to progress towards general management, but that he was better suited for a more specialist role.

Career drivers

A career driver is an 'inner force which determines what you want and what you need from your working life' (Francis, 1985). One well-known approach to career drivers comes from the work of Schein (1978). He described eight 'career anchors', listed in Box 5.2. Schein suggests that a career anchor provides a steadying influence for a person, providing a pivot around which the less favoured anchors can revolve.

Box 5.2 Schein's career anchors

- Technical-functional – a need to be valued for specialist skills.
- General management – a need to have responsibility for people.
- Autonomy and independence – a need to be free of bureaucratic constraints.
- Entrepreneurial creativity – a need to create an original 'enterprise'.
- Security – a need for continuity of employment.
- Service orientation – a need to serve and 'improve the world'.
- Challenge – a need to self-test.
- Lifestyle – a need to attain balance between work and non-work.

A questionnaire yields scores, which point to possible key career anchors. These results should be explored, along with any themes arising from other exercises.

Another questionnaire which provides a basis for discussing career drivers was detailed in Francis (1985) and is set out in Box 5.3.

Box 5.3 Career drivers (Francis)

- Material rewards – seeking possession, wealth and a high standard of living.
- Power and influence – seeking to be in control of people and resources.
- Search for meaning – seeking to do things believed to be valuable for their own sake.

(Continued)

(Continued)

- Expertise – seeking a high level of accomplishment in a specialised field.
- Creativity – seeking to innovate and be identified with original input.
- Affiliation – seeking nourishing relationships with others at work.
- Autonomy – seeking to be independent and make key decisions for oneself.
- Status – seeking to be recognised, admired and respected by the community at large.
- Security – seeking a solid and predictable future.

Dangers of using tests in career counselling

Excessive emphasis on test interpretation

It is, unfortunately, attractive for career counsellors to show off their 'expertise' by using interpretations with which they are familiar, but which have little meaning for the client. Such an excessive emphasis on interpretation is unlikely to allow the expression of the client's feelings about the results. Furthermore, this will discourage a client from being proactive and encourage passivity.

It is important to reiterate that any assessment tools used in career counselling are proferred as resources to aid self-assessment. Inevitably, some clients will *want* to read more into test results than is warranted. The counsellor should then be careful to place the results in context, and refer to the client's self-perceptions as the primary focus for discussion.

Occasionally it may be necessary to make light of the tests with a comment such as, 'These questionnaires are, after all, only feeding back to you what you have put into them, but in a structured format.'

Every care must be taken not to misuse the power and trust invested in the counsellor.

Tests dominating the counselling

Clients can be very gullible and naive regarding the acceptance of test results, and it can be seductive to allow tests to dominate the discussions. This is especially true when there is a lack of time available, because of pressures to see a large number of clients. Insufficient training of counsellors can also lead to an excessive reliance on what, after all, are only partly accurate results. The British Psychological Society has rightly brought in a Certificate of Occupational Testing, which may go some way to reducing the misuse of those insufficiently validated and unreliable instruments now on the market which may be seen by clients as 'proper tests'.

Other client characteristics, such as lack of interest in pursuing the discussion of 'problems', in favour of a 'quick-fix solution' can pressure counsellors into relying too much on test results. After all, clients have a right to their results, may be looking forward expectantly to receiving them, and might, unless sufficiently forewarned in initial contracting, secretly hope for some magical answers to emerge.

Tests are not appropriate for every person

Even if a test has been properly validated (that is, the test has been shown to be measuring what it says, within certain statistical margins of error), it may not be sufficiently appropriate for a particular client. This could be because the client:

- does not fully understand the questions, perhaps because English is not their first language;
- answers the questions randomly;
- does not feel well on the day of testing; or
- wants to make a particular impression.

Confusion of interests and abilities

Being good at something does not guarantee an interest in the subject. It can be too easily assumed by clients that a so-called high score on an 'interests inventory' means that a client will be 'good' at the activity or occupation. Similarly, a high score on an aptitude test does not necessarily mean an equally high level of interest.

Managing a feedback session

Because clients place great store on 'results', especially of any aptitude or ability testing, any feedback session must take account of this if it is to be helpful. Career counsellors not only need adequate training in the development and ethical use of tests, but also in how they can be integrated effectively into the career counselling process.

Chapter 3 (see p. 43) underlined the importance of establishing, at the outset, the position of any exercise as *part* of the 'exploring' and 'clarifying' stages of career counselling. In addition, it is always useful to remind clients at the beginning of a feedback session of the purpose of the meeting, its place in the whole career counselling process, and the role any exercise, questionnaire or test is to play in it. For example: 'They can enable us to focus our discussion on important areas relevant to the career counselling goals we set at the first meeting. At the end of our session, I'll give you a few more exercises to help move you on to the next stage – then next time we meet, we can review your reflections, focus on ideas, and move towards some kind of action.'

Because we want to encourage client ownership, we usually start a feedback discussion with any home assignments (see pp. 51–2) which the client has addressed. Inevitably, client reactions to the exercises will vary, but they often find them thought-provoking and quite difficult; for example, the exercise 'Satisfying Achievments' (see p. 55 and p. 167) challenges clients to complete a virtually blank sheet of paper, and decide what constitutes 'an achievement' in their eyes. It is important to avoid conveying any sense of disapproval if a client has not 'completed' an exercise. They may have thought long and hard about it, but could not find the will or the words to commit their thoughts to paper. Talking it through may well help:

Dave:	I haven't had the time to do all these exercises.
Career counsellor (Cc):	You've been really busy then.
Dave:	Yes, and I just couldn't think how to start.
Cc:	So the questions were hard?
Dave:	No ... I mean yes ... well, I don't think I've ever achieved anything.
Cc:	Yes, 'achievement' is a strong word.
Dave:	Hmm ... well, there *have* been some good times.
Cc:	Can I hear about one of them?

Other clients may have completed the exercises in great detail, and done a good deal of analysis on any patterns arising. It is the individual's response to the exercises that is useful to bring out in the session, as well as the details of the examples chosen by the client. Some clients will certainly need support to 'bring alive' a particular event; others will value the career counsellor's thoughts on apparent patterns additional to those they have already identified.

As with any exercise the client has undertaken, it is helpful to gauge the client's response to a test or questionnaire by asking how they found it. This helps to engage the client in discussing the results openly, and minimises any defensiveness about the results. When using a test or questionnaire with 'scores', it is important to explain that the results are only a guide, and, in the case of a personality or preference questionnaire, simply represent the client's self-perception at this particular point in time. This tends to de-mystify the tests, and focuses attention on the individual; the task of the session is to help the client begin to make sense of the results (they can continue to do this by listening to a tape of the session, and discussing it with a trusted third party).

Once the purpose of a particular test or questionnaire has been explained, it can be beneficial to ask clients to 'estimate' how they imagine they scored. After initial surprise, clients often become very engaged with this approach, and the subsequent discussion can focus on the client's reaction to the *difference* between their self-perception and the score, rather than just on the scores themselves.

At the end of the feedback discussion, it can be useful to ask the client to summarise the key issues that have struck them, and how they feel about the session. Then, it is appropriate to give further home assignments.

Tape-recording the feedback discussions

Because tests provide a large volume of information which clients then have to sift through and integrate into their own self-assessment, we have found that tape-recording the feedback discussion has enormous benefits:

- It provides a live record of an important and unique interaction for the client.
- It can be listened to days, weeks, months or even years after the actual meeting – a 'live' reminder of a meeting at an important time in the client's life. Some clients have remarked, years later, how they have changed over time, although it is always a good idea to caution them that the career counselling they experienced was predominantly a 'snapshot' in time.
- It can be shared with a significant other person.
- It diminishes the emphasis on the 'pieces of paper' (the results).
- It enables the client to hear more of what was discussed at a time when he or she is not so closely involved.

Clients can be asked to bring their own tape to the meeting, while the career counsellor provides the recording equipment. This clarifies that the client rather than the counsellor 'owns' the tape, that is, that the test results are the client's rather than the counsellor's property.

Whilst taping has a lot to recommend it, it is important for the career counsellor to be comfortable with the idea, and for the client to be given encouragement to accept taping, but also the freedom to reject it. It must be made clear that any taping of sessions is also part of the confidentiality agreement of the career counselling.

Clients' thinking often moves forward considerably following a test feedback session. Many thoughts, feelings and ideas are triggered by listening to the tape. Some reactions not obviously connected with the career counselling may come up when clients listen to their tapes. Comments on voice production are quite often made; for example, 'I never realised I sounded like that' (loud, quiet, aggressive, talkative, negative). Some of these comments can provide useful data for counselling.

Once a tape has been made, it can be used to stimulate the client to prepare for the next meeting. Clients can be asked to write their reflections, thoughts, ideas and feelings on listening to the tape. They may also want to share the tape with someone close to them, or a person involved in their decision making. To encourage a continuing active role in the career counselling, clients can be asked to complete the summary chart (see p. 59) and 'Job satisfiers' exercise (see pp. 63–4 and pp. 168–9). To synthesise their thoughts on paper in this way can help to clarify significantly what may previously have been a jumble of disconnected thoughts and reflections.

The benefits of taping are consistent with the values of counselling which encourage clients to take responsibility for their own decisions. As much as anything else, taping can help to further client self-understanding as a preparation for action.

Using occupational information

By this stage of the career counselling process, clients should have been disabused of any notion that the career counsellor is a matchmaker, that is, a person who will translate information about the client into the perfect 'career match', and who will know all there is to know about that occupation (and all others too). However, in order to make a decision about what course of action to pursue, the client does need information about options (for example, education and training, related career options, job opportunities, career pathways within an organisation, alternatives to traditional careers). Clients need information about what they would like to do (given their interests, personality and values) and what they can do (with their capabilities, skills and qualifications). Good information will enable the client to assess him- or herself in relation to various options.

Many career counsellors feel anxious about the topic of occupational information. This is understandable: there is a bewildering amount of occupational information available, of varying quality, in various media and from a variety of sources. With the best will in the world, it is just not possible to keep abreast of all the information about career possibilities. The accessibility of so much information on the Internet has certainly eased the research task for both client and career counsellor. The lack of its categorisation, however, means that such information must be approached with a clear framework and focus.

We believe that it is more realistic to consider the career counsellor as a 'general practitioner' with respect to knowledge of the world of work. Familiarity with job classification families, levels of entry and types of educational/training opportunities is important (see Boxes 5.5, 5.6 and 5.7).

Career counsellors should also have a knowledge of how to access information. Like a general practitioner, at times it will be necessary to refer clients to 'consultants', people who have detailed knowledge of particular careers. Appendix C lists a number of sources of occupational information.

The role of information

Information may be particularly appropriate when:

- clients need to consider the realism of their ideas, in terms of entry requirements (for example, 'Am I qualified to train as a solicitor?');
- clients feel constrained within an occupation (for example, 'What else can a teacher do except teach?');
- clients have narrow ideas and want to broaden their horizons (for example, 'I've always worked with animals – what other careers are there?');
- clients' ideas are dictated by glamorous or romantic notions (for example, 'What is it really like to work in the travel industry?'); or
- clients need to develop more confidence in the suitability of an occupation before embarking on training (for example, 'Is physiotherapy suitable for me?').

It is helpful to consider information which the client may already possess, and which may act as a block to considering other options. The individual's socio-economic background can be a key determinant of this:

Julie was a languages graduate; her father was a security guard and her mother a cleaner. She was the first person from her family to go to university. During her third year, she panicked about her choice of career. Occupations where she could make direct use of her languages, such as interpreting or publishing, seemed very mysterious. She eventually went into teaching, not because the job had any real appeal, but because she was familiar with it, having been in a classroom herself. Interpreting and publishing felt like 'worlds apart'. She came for career counselling after she failed her first teaching practice.

A young man from an upper-class professional background who wants to enter a manual trade will be at as much of a disadvantage as Julie, who had no family tradition of professional work on which to draw when considering future options.

Generally, it is appropriate to encourage clients to broaden their ideas about occupational possibilities and cast a wide net initially, before narrowing down the options and assessing a 'shortlist' in detail.

Helping the client to generate options

Many clients will need support to think of ideas 'out of the box'. We find it useful to give clients an exercise to act as a framework for generating initial ideas prior to a joint 'brainstorming' session. Clients are encouraged to use their 'Job satisfiers' and summary exercises to focus their ideas, but otherwise to keep an open mind. We encourage them to 'pay attention' to the jobs people do all around them – friends, neighbours and anyone they come into contact with on a daily basis, and to look at some recommended websites and appropriate careers directories (see Appendix C). Sometimes it may be useful to give the client a careers classification, such as the Careers Library Classification Index (CLCI) used in careers libraries and in some directories of occupational information. Another is John Holland's categories (Holland, 1983), to which we referred earlier (see pp. 75–7). These schemes can broaden ideas: for example in the CLCI, looking up 'banking' will lead the client to section N, where information on other careers in finance will also be found.

To help clients think creatively, try to develop a light-hearted approach. Some methods are listed in Box 5.4. The client then categorises the ideas into 'similar', 'complementary' and 'breakthrough' in relation to current or previous work. Then they do a 'pros and cons' analysis on their shortlist.

Box 5.4 Suggestions for generating career options

- Recall memories of early ambitions.
- Draw your ideal job situation and then look at what it represents.
- Circle job ads that appeal.
- List jobs of every friend/relative/neighbour you know and choose six that have some appeal.
- Highlight jobs that appeal in the index of a careers directory (*Job file*, *Occupations*, etc.: see 'Reference books' in Appendix C).
- Brainstorm ideas with a friend/colleague/career counsellor.
- Ask everyone you know for ideas about what they could see you doing.
- Look up articles in careers reference books for all the ideas you have had – *Occupations* gives lists of similar careers, for example, a client who is interested in architecture will find civil engineering, surveying and landscape architecture suggested.
- For a week, as you watch television or see other people at work, note down jobs that appeal to you.
- Consider creative alternatives too, for example, self-employment, franchising, voluntary work, combining two part-time occupations (such as teaching and writing).

Jan (see p. 63) based her job ideas preparation on two key factors: she would think of jobs that included more contact with people and front-line work, rather than back-room research. Her listed included market research, employment research, information manager (NHS) and systems analyst (see pp. 93–4).

What information does the career counsellor need?

Career counsellors should know about sources of information (see Appendix C) and have at least a general knowledge of careers, for example, of job areas, levels of entry and the types of training and education which are available. Box 5.5 lists 'families' into which jobs can be classified. Rather than knowing about every course in existence, career counsellors should be familiar with types of training and education opportunities; Box 5.6 provides a list.

Box 5.5 Job areas

- Armed Forces
- Administration, business, clerical and management
- Art, craft and design
- Teaching and cultural activities
- Entertainment and leisure
- Hospitality, catering and other services
- Health and medical services
- Social and related services
- Law and related work
- Security and protective services
- Finance and related work
- Buying, selling and related services
- Sciences, mathematics and related work
- Engineering
- Manufacturing industries
- Construction and land services
- Animals, plants and the environment
- Transport

Source: From Occupations published annually by the DfES.

Box 5.6 Training and education opportunities

- Adult residential course
- Distance or open learning courses
- Day and evening adult education colleges
- Courses focusing on minority group interests
- 'Return to learn' and 'ready to work' courses
- Courses attracting government funding
- Institutions of higher education welcoming mature students
- Occupations particularly amenable to retraining
- Local employment, retraining and education opportunities
- Sources of funding for grants and loans
- Details of education advisory agencies (e.g. Learndirect)
- Details of other local advisory agencies (e.g. Learning and Skills Council's Business Link for free business advice and training)

Non-written sources of occupational information

The most valuable source of occupational information is clients' first-hand work experience (which will inevitably be limited). Reference books can only give factual information (see Box 5.7) rather than a real flavour of the work.

Box 5.7 Categories of information found in reference books

- What the work involves
- Typical working environment
- Pay and conditions
- Opportunities
- Prospects
- Personal attributes required
- Qualifications required for entry
- Training
- Late entry
- Related careers
- Opportunities for part-time work or career breaks
- Addresses for further information (professional bodies etc.)

'Psychosocial' information is occupational information which gives more of an idea of what the job is really like than the information found in books and pamphlets. The kinds of question not usually addressed in careers books include:

- How is the same occupation different in a small rather than a large organisation? (For example, a woman administrator who needed power and influence realised that she would be more likely to achieve this in a small organisation.)
- How will the company or career culture fit in with the individual's identity? (For example, a mechanical engineer who was gay felt very uncomfortable in a macho environment.)
- How will the requirements of a job affect both partners in a relationship? (For example, a firefighter married a woman who could not come to terms with the degree of risk involved.)
- What are the patterns of interaction with others? (For example, a secretary who was promoted to the position of office manager found that her friendships with the people who were no longer her peers were affected.)
- What is the occupational lifestyle, and will it allow the client to have the overall lifestyle he or she wants? (For example, occupations involving evening or week-end work are likely to cause difficulties for a person who plays competitive tennis.)

This information is more difficult to pin down – it is most likely to be found in other people's heads! There are complexities because occupational experiences are so variable that many different patterns of needs, personalities and lifestyle preferences can be satisfied. For example, within the occupation of counsellor, some people work as a member of a team, others in isolation, with no colleague support; some have relatively brief or superficial contact with lots of people; others have intensive, long-term relationships with a very small number of clients. Here are some methods of obtaining psychosocial information:

1   Visits, observation, work shadowing, voluntary, part-time or temporary experience.

Joseph was interested in physiotherapy and wanted to know more about whether it would suit his personality. He arranged to do some voluntary work in a hospital, and visited the physiotherapy department. He spent two days 'shadowing' a physiothera-pist at work, and asked a lot of questions. After discussing the experience with his counsellor, he decided to apply for training.

2   Interviewing a person in an occupation.

Freddie had had a successful experience of teaching his wife to drive, and wondered about becoming a driving instructor. He arranged to talk to a driving instructor about the work and, with the help of his counsellor, prepared a list of questions to use as a basis for interviewing her. He did this by using his 'Job satisfiers' exercise (see p. 63) to generate questions *related to* the satisfiers. For example, one of his top job satisfiers was 'a need for some autonomy – I must be able to control the way I work much of the time.' This led to the question: 'How much of the way you teach is prescribed, and how much do you decide?'

Some examples of general questions for clients to ask are listed in Box 5.8.

Box 5.8 Information interviewing

Examples of questions:

- Why did you choose this as a career?
- What is a typical day like?
- What do you consider to be a 'good' day – and a 'bad' one?
- How many people do you meet in an average week? What types of people?
- What do you like best about the job? What is most rewarding?
- What do you like least about the job? What is most stressful?
- If you could change the job to give you more job satisfaction, what changes would you make?
- How does the job affect your life outside work?

In his next session with the counsellor, Freddie said that he had been very struck by what the driving instructor had said about coping with nervous drivers and the need for patience. It appeared that his wife was a 'born driver' and had made rapid progress, passing her test at the first attempt. He felt that he would not enjoy dealing with people who were 'failures', and decided to abandon the idea.

3   Professional bodies/trade associations – for example, the Law Society for information about legal careers.
4   Personal contacts: parents, partners, relatives, colleagues, ex-colleagues and friends (together with *their* contacts) may be valuable sources of occupational information. Generally, the further away information gets 'from the horse's mouth', the less valuable it becomes.

Occupational information: guidelines for the career counsellor

1   Ensure that clients understand that they are responsible for doing their own research. This should have been stated at the contracting stage (see Chapter 3). Research is not a clinical process – it is vital that clients 'own' this part of the process, but also know what resources are available, and how to access them.
2   Avoid using the career counselling session as a vehicle for feeding information to a client. There is a danger of confusing the contract.
3   Show clients how to generate a list of career possibilities.
4   Help clients to address the questions 'What information do I need? and 'Where or how can I get it?'
5   Direct clients to relevant formal and written sources of information which are likely to be dispassionate and objective, and also to informal, oral sources where possible.
6   Encourage and support clients in the process of researching career options in detail.
7   Help clients to relate the occupational information as objectively as possible to the results of career counselling. For example, a client who is very attracted to being a solicitor but not very articulate may try to persuade himself that he is articulate when he reads that this is one of the qualities required. It may be helpful to give the client some questions to pose when researching. For example, 'What is or seems to fit who I am?' and 'Could I see myself becoming this?'
8   Help clients to evaluate the information, and caution them about the inaccuracy or incompleteness of some information. For example, most occupational information is geared to school leavers, and entry requirements may be different in practice for mature entrants.
9   Support clients in dealing with their emotional reactions when gathering information. Prepare them to expect a variety of positive and negative emotions. Some clients will need further support as they meet hurdles or setbacks.

Researching occupational information may produce surprising insights for a client, and lead to a revision of the self-concept:

Carolyn had been working as a sales representative and was considering training as a social worker, until she did some investigation into the level of student grant and of starting salaries when qualified. She had not expected the work to be well paid, but was very shocked when she realised the sacrifices which would be involved if she was to pursue this career. She also needed support to talk through her discovery of how important economic values actually were to her when it came to the crunch.

Employment market information

The Government has made employment market information available online. For people not wanting to use the web, the Government publishes *Labour Market Trends* monthly, and this can be accessed at reference libraries. For more detailed information (for example, on employment trends in a particular occupation) we would recommend approaching the representative body for that occupation. Information from these sources may be more anecdotal, but it will be more specific. See Appendix C for names of specific websites.

Information about employment trends and forecasts of shortage occupations dates very rapidly and is not widely available in reference books. Occasional reports are produced, for example, by the Skills and Enterprise Network, but information is best obtained from more ephemeral sources such as newspaper articles or from interviewing experts rather than from books. It can also be misleading. Trends do not last; people who decide to train in a shortage occupation now may find that by the time they are qualified, there is a glut.

In addition, generalisations about declining sectors do not necessarily mean that a particular client will not be successful in applying for a position in such a sector. Clearly, success is more likely if the client is well motivated, competent, has good job-hunting skills and is prepared to relocate.

Summary

This chapter has considered how the use of psychometric tests and other questionnaires can add richness, clarity and validity to the information generated from home assignments, described in Chapter 4. It has also indicated how important it is to integrate any tests into the overall career counselling contract. We have also looked at how researching the requirements of occupations can enable clients to relate their self-understanding to work possibilities. We have stressed the importance of ensuring that such techniques, and particularly the interpretation of test results, are used in a way which is consistent with the values of counselling, where clients are responsible for decision making.

The final phase of the career counselling process, enabling clients to use their enhanced self-understanding to make decisions and formulate action plans, is addressed in Chapter 6. Endings, support and follow-up will also be discussed.

Checklist: Using tests, questionnaires and occupational information

☑ When introducing any exercise which could be viewed by a client as a 'test', ensure you position it as just one part of the whole process of gathering information for the client to reflect on.

☑ Use tests together with questionnaires and home assignments.

(Continued)

(Continued)

☑ Only give a 'test' to a client *after* you have met, and decided together that it will be suitable for this individual.

☑ Ensure that you have not just the training to use a test, but also the *time* to discuss and integrate it into the career counselling.

☑ Don't give in to pressure from clients wanting a test as a 'quick fix'.

☑ Remember you don't have to know everything about every occupation.

☑ Consider yourself as a 'resource of resources' – point clients in the direction of the sources of information they need.

☑ Use information to help clients broaden their horizons, as well as to check out the realism of their ideas.

☑ Encourage clients to use reference books and websites as a starting point, and then to meet with people working in the jobs of interest.

☑ Coach clients in the preparation of questions relevant to their job satisfiers prior to an 'information-seeking' meeting.

6 Action, Outcomes and Endings

This chapter extends the discussion of techniques of promoting self-understanding to the final phase, the point when clients are ready to end the career counselling relationship, either temporarily or permanently.

The use of scaling techniques from solution-focused therapy and coaching is again useful at this stage (see also p. 61 and p. 99) and will be described, together with ways of agreeing tangible objectives and action plans.

The closer clients come to a decision, the more they may experience and show 'resistance'. The feelings associated with such resistance and ways of enabling clients to address their dilemmas will be discussed, together with exercises to assist clients in moving towards a decision.

The career counselling process does not necessarily end at the final meeting, although the progress clients have made towards meeting their objectives for the career counselling can and should be reviewed at this stage. Ways of encouraging clients to maintain momentum will also be discussed.

Decision making and action

Counsellor and client have reached the final phase of the career counselling. Good contracting earlier on will be of great value now. It is likely, however, that whatever was contracted earlier, the client will come expecting to 'move on' in some way and to end this stage of the career counselling with something tangible to take away.

It makes some sense to recognise the inevitability of the 'ending' in the original contracting and subsequent meetings. A challenge for career counsellors and clients is to move effectively from the 'exploring' and 'clarifying' stages to the motivation needed for effective action. In our experience, it makes sense for clients to appreciate, even at the early stages of career counselling, the kind of outcomes or actions that could result. This knowledge may enable them to be better prepared, and therefore motivated for, the inevitable time when the career counselling ends.

What is action?
The word 'action' is somewhat limiting in describing this stage. What gives meaning to 'action' will be defined by the goals of career counselling set out in the original contract. Thus, an employer-sponsored client may define action as 'deciding whether to go for a partnership or director role or to stay in a more specialist, functional position'. On the other hand, a self-sponsored client might expect that the choice is either

between, resignedly, staying put in the current career, or making a complete change of career. Box 6.1 indicates the variety of actions that can take place.

Box 6.1 Varieties of actions

- Change attitude and approach to current job.
- Increase self-expression outside work (for example, take up writing/art).
- Seek development within organisation (for example, secondment, project work, job rotation, becoming a mentor or coach).
- Change department, but to a similar job.
- Change position within the organisation (for example, from functional to management role).
- Change organisation, but stay in same career.
- Change from full-time to part-time or freelance employment (possibly developing a new career in spare time).
- Take a sabbatical.
- Take on two part-time positions.
- Start own business in spare time (perhaps extending a hobby).
- Take new job as a 'stepping stone' to new career – for example (a) within the organisation: sales to marketing; (b) outside the organisation: from banking to public relations via financial public relations.
- Change career by retraining (for example, Open University MBA).
- Change career by promoting transferable skills (for example, teacher to trainer).

Some of these changes may affect each other; for example, increasing the emphasis placed on life outside work may decrease the discomfort felt in work. Clients may not be fully aware of the possibilities available to them. Showing them Box 6.1 might succeed in prompting greater awareness and a more creative approach to thinking about the future. This could even be done at the contracting stage; a useful question to ask clients is 'What do you imagine the different possible outcomes from our work together might be?' (See Chapter 3, 'Screening, Contracting and Exploring'.)

Many clients will want at least to consider alternative career scenarios, even if they end up rejecting them. The counsellor can enable clients to do this by giving written assignments, which can aid the consideration of options and enable a decision to be made.

Choosing between options: written exercises

The first exercise – 'Satisfiers vs. options' – is appropriate to give at the time when the counsellor senses that clients are in a position to make a sufficiently rational assessment of what they want in a job. If this is not the case, the 'Guided fantasy' exercise described later in this chapter is more suitable. 'Guided fantasy' may also suit clients who respond to a more intuitive approach. The other exercises in this section may be useful in coming to a decision about a possible option which has been identified through the first exercise.

These exercises have several benefits:

- Clients may reflect and move forward on their own, independently of the career counsellor.
- Clients may produce their own ideas for discussion, thereby reducing the chances of becoming embroiled in a 'Why don't you …?', 'Yes, but …' discussion.
- Clients may become more motivated to overcome hurdles to implementation.
- The degree of thought and research put in by clients provides the counsellor with some clues to progress and the approach required in the final meeting (for example, is further counselling required? Does the client want to discuss practicalities?)

'Satisfiers vs. options'

The purpose of this exercise is to provide clients with a framework for considering possible options for the future, and to prompt them to start assessing the degree of satisfaction they might provide. The exercise asks for the list of elements of job satisfaction produced in the 'Job satisfiers' exercise (see p. 63) to be evaluated against a number of scenarios.

Box 6.2 'Satisfiers vs. options': Jan's ratings

Job satisfiers

Options	1	2	3	4	5	6	7	8	9	10	11	12	Total
Last job	7	10	7	9	8	4	9	1	6	4	2	2	69
Same occupation, different organisation	9	9	9	10	9	10	5	10	9	8	9	7	104
Previous job (for comparison)	5	2	9	10	3	8	2	10	3	8	7	6	73
Market research	5	6	6	6	5	5	4	6	8	7	8	7	73
Employment research	7	10	7	7	6	6	9	7	5	7	6	7	84
Academic research	7	10	6	7	7	6	9	6	4	8	5	6	81
Info. manager (NHS)	7	9	10	10	9	9	6	10	8	7	9	9	103
Info. manager (education)	7	9	10	10	9	10	6	10	8	7	9	7	102
Systems analyst	7	9	8	9	10	7	6	10	8	8	7	7	96
Self-employment (consultancy)	8	9	10	9	7	4	10	9	6	10	8	8	98

(Continued)

(Continued)

Key to job satisfiers

1 Intellectual stimulation	7 Freedom to set own schedule
2 Using analytical skills	8 Responding to a felt need
3 Using oral/written communication skills	9 Impact on decision making
	10 Organisation values high standards
4 Using organisational skills	11 Visible, central (not backroom) role
5 Solving complex problems	12 Innovative, progressive environment
6 Collaborating with colleagues	

Clients are asked, for each possible option they are considering, to rate on a 1 to 10 scale the extent to which they believe each option would offer them job satisfaction (1 = not at all; 10 = complete satisfaction). It can also be useful (if possible) for the client to include their current job, a previous job they have enjoyed and a previous job they have disliked, for comparison purposes. Box 6.2 shows Jan's completed matrix (see p. 63 for her case study).

At this stage generating energy and being creative is more important than being precise. During the rating process, clients can be encouraged to give their subjective evaluations freely – even if they do not have completely accurate information about an option, they can make an estimate. Scenarios which the client rates are likely to include different careers, but need not be restricted to alternative career choices. They may include any of the suggestions in Box 6.3.

Box 6.3 Possible scenarios for 'Satisfiers vs. options' exercise

- Alternative career, while in training
- Alternative career, one year after training
- Alternative career, five years after training
- A combination of two activities (for example, development of creative writing while continuing in current career)
- Two part-time jobs
- Self-employment (after six months, two years, five years)
- A 'stepping-stone' job
- Current role with a different boss
- Current occupation with a different employer
- Current role with 'development'
- New role with the current employer

Other possible options may arise during counselling.

Pros and cons

When at least one reasonably attractive option has been identified, a simple 'Pros and cons' exercise (Box 6.4) can assist clients to consider the practical long- and short-term advantages of that option. The questions implicit in this exercise are:

- Of what benefit would this option be to me?
- What would I have to give up to pursue this option?
- How likely is it that I could achieve this option, given my constraints and assets?

Box 6.4 Angela's 'Pros and cons' exercise sheet

OPTION: Law (training to be a solicitor)

	Pros	Cons
Short term	In London	Low income
	Be with husband	Difficult to find traineeship
	The training	Low pay
Long term	Professional	Might not find
	qualification	type of work want
	Be a partner	Need to take work home
	Potential earnings	Too office-bound

Balance sheet

This exercise enables clients to focus on the effects of making a particular choice on the important people in and aspects of their lives. Both negative and positive effects are examined, as demonstrated in Box 6.5.

Box 6.5 Freddie's 'Balance sheet' exercise

OPTION: Start small business in spare time

Effects on	Negative	Positive
Wife	She may resent losing some of our quality time	She has said I need something to lift me
Children	Less time to play	They could earn some pocket money
Employer	I won't be available as before on Fridays May get overtired	I may be able to supply the company
Health		Will get less depressed
Finances	Less money in short term	Possibly more in long term

In all of these exercises, it is possible to add some refinement to the preferences and consequences by weighting each of them, for example, on a scale of 1 to 5 in terms of their importance.

'Optimist vs. pessimist'

This exercise asks clients to have a dialogue between the optimistic and pessimistic parts of themselves. When a client seems to be 'in two minds' about a course of action, saying something like 'I know this is right for me, but I can't seem to bring myself to do it', the 'Optimist vs. pessimist' exercise may be useful in helping clients to uncover any attitudes which may be blocking them from making a decision and to address any anxieties which may be preventing them from taking constructive action. See Box 6.6 for an example.

Box 6.6 Kathy's 'Optimist vs. pessimist' exercise

COURSE OF ACTION: Start a correspondence course in journalism

Optimist: I can do this because: I have an aptitude for writing.
Pessimist: I can't do this because: I'm afraid of my writing being criticised.
Optimist: I can do this because: I have a lot of support and encouragement at home.
Pessimist: I can't do this because: I'm too busy at work.
Optimist: I can do this because: I know about time management and prioritising, and learning journalism is very important to me.

The exercise can be carried out either in writing or face to face. If conducting the exercise face to face, ask the client to acknowledge that two sides exist – the part that expects things to work out fine, and the part that expects the worst to happen. If using the written approach, follow it up with a discussion about the themes that seem to be holding the client back.

Reviewing and evaluating progress

Towards the end of career counselling, a progress review enables both the client and counsellor to look back at what has been achieved. A review may serve the following purposes:

- It paves the way for ending the relationship, and prepares clients to continue their journey without the counsellor.
- It enables the client to see the career counselling in perspective.
- It strengthens the client's resolve and confidence, by highlighting the progress made.
- It underlines clients' continuing responsibility for their own development.

Although the primary objective of a review is not the evaluation of the counsellor's work, the review process may also give useful feedback to the counsellor about their work. (The evaluation of career counselling is discussed in Chapter 9.)

We have found that the feedback from progress reviews fits Oakeshott's (1991) model, which was developed in an educational guidance context, that the helping process enables clients to increase their knowledge and self-awareness and acquire a number of personal skills. These include decision-making and action-planning skills, self-confidence, and goal-setting techniques. This confirms our view that the career counselling process is educative.

It is helpful to ask clients to recall the objectives with which they began career counselling, although these may have changed as clients progressed through the stages. Generally, many clients begin career counselling by articulating externally observable objectives, for example, gaining information about options. The process of review can reveal that, although clients do make some progress towards achieving such objectives, change at a more subtle level has occurred. Allen (1975) describes these as changes in:

- internal cognitive functioning – for example, an increased understanding of behaviour and the reasons for it, and fewer self-limiting beliefs; and
- internal affective functioning – for example, coping more effectively with negative feelings, such as anger and bitterness about redundancy, or developing greater self-confidence.

One client expressed surprise at the boost in her self-confidence:

> Career counselling channelled me into thinking about what I really enjoyed and was good at. The whole experience of guided self-examination has, to my surprise, given me a lot more confidence about actually going for what I want.

These more subtle, or internal, changes may take time to work through to (external) action, and may not be immediately visible to others. Pressure can be created for clients by well-meaning friends and relatives, who may look for tangible signs of the success of career counselling. For example, 'Well, what was the result then? – What are you going to *do*?' Good career counselling will incorporate into goals and action ways to respond to significant others, as well as targets and 'rewards' to recognise progress (see also p. 107).

Goals and action steps

There is often a confusion between the terms 'goal' and 'action'. Goals are specific statements of *what* clients aim to achieve. Action planning is *how* clients will set about achieving their goals. The temptation to rush on to the 'how' without sufficiently considering the 'what' should be resisted.

Establishing useful goals is not an easy process. An effective goal will conform to a number of criteria, summarised by the mnemonic SMART:

Specific
Measurable
Attractive
Realistic
Time-bound

- *Specific*   Goals are virtually useless if stated in general terms. They are likely to be as effective as a New Year resolution like 'I must give up smoking.' On the other hand, it helps to start somewhere. The counsellor can help clients to increase the specificity of a 'statement of intent' by asking the single question 'How?'. Box 6.7 gives an example of the three steps towards converting a vague statement of intent into a more specific aim and then into a very specific goal.

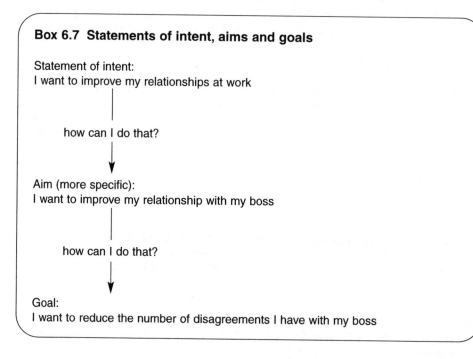

Box 6.7 Statements of intent, aims and goals

Statement of intent:
I want to improve my relationships at work

how can I do that?

Aim (more specific):
I want to improve my relationship with my boss

how can I do that?

Goal:
I want to reduce the number of disagreements I have with my boss

- *Measurable*   In addition to being specific, the goal should be measurable or verifiable. In other words, 'I will know I have achieved it when [for example] I have reduced the number of disagreements I have with my boss.'
- *Attractive*   An attractive goal is one to which clients are committed. If the goal is for someone else, or there is another more important goal behind the one expressed, this goal will be sabotaged. An example is when clients express a desire to earn more money, whereas the hidden goal is to gain more recognition. A goal aimed at increasing salary alone may not bring the required recognition.
- *Realistic*   Goals should not be rooted in fantasy, thus being too difficult to achieve. Nor should they be so easy to attain that clients are hardly motivated to act. Goals *should* be within the client's value system, and of sufficient significance to provide a reward on their completion.
- *Time-bound*   Setting some time limit for achievement of goals provides a focus. Such time boundaries can act as motivators in themselves. They can also act as review dates.

See the exercise on 'Setting objectives' in Appendix H.

Using scaling techniques

Solution-focused coaching makes frequent use of 'scaling' (see also Chapter 4, pp. 61–2). At this stage of the career counselling, the career counsellor can use a scale of 1 to 10 to check both the attractiveness and realism of clients' goals.

Justin set himself this goal: 'To become Research and Development Director of my company within 18 months.' His career counsellor asked him: 'How attractive is this goal to you on a scale of 1 to 10?'

Justin:	Eight.
Career counsellor (Cc):	So what would move it one point up the scale to nine?
Justin:	If the company goes ahead with the planned relocation.
Cc:	So how realistic is the goal, Justin, on the 1 to 10 scale?
Justin:	Probably a six or seven.
Cc:	So what tells you it's a six or seven, and not lower, say at three or four?
Justin:	Well, I've had feedback that I'm considered a good candidate, and I'd really love the job.
Cc:	And to get to an eight or nine?
Justin:	I'd need to convince one or two more key players that I am the right man for the job. Also, my wife will need to be on board, as I'd be away from home more often. ...

The action plan

Once a good enough goal has been agreed, the client can be encouraged to think about the steps he or she needs to take to achieve it. A written action plan can be a useful way of clarifying clients' stated commitments to action, and a suggested pro-forma which can be useful to clients is given in Appendix B. There is always the danger, however, that clients will prematurely decide on an action plan without sufficient thought, either to please the counsellor or to convince themselves or a significant other person, such as a partner or a parent, that a decision has been reached.

The very act of completing such a plan on paper, after what has probably been an intense and introspective experience, can act as both a tangible reward and a spur to action. But there is a greater likelihood that action plans will be successful if the counsellor ensures that the criteria shown in Box 6.8 are first met.

Box 6.8 Criteria to fulfil before completing action plans

- Identify well-thought-out goals.
- Allow action plan to be owned by client.
- Indicate to client that action plan is not rigid, should be reviewed regularly, and probably revised.
- Give sufficient time to address fears of change.
- Address ways of coping with disappointment.

See also the exercise on 'Action planning' in Appendix H.

Addressing fears of change

> All changes, even the most longed for, have their melancholy, for what we leave behind us is a part of ourselves; we must die to one life before we can accept another. (Anatole France, *The Crime of Sylvestre Bonnard*)

It should come as no surprise that clients show anxiety when approaching what they consider the 'crunch point' – a decision just has to be made. Of course, some of the techniques and exercises already described can help to reduce such anxiety or at least make it more tolerable. There are a number of contributory factors to the 'cold feet' many clients have at this point.

Clients may worry that their choice may not meet with the approval of significant others. Possibly because of past experiences of rejection, they may fear competition in the job market. There may be fears that the plan will not work (for example, a shy client who finds it hard to ask for information). Apparent 'cold feet' about making a career decision may be due to the client's decision, on reflection, that other life issues take priority (for example, adjusting to a divorce).

Further counselling may be necessary before clients are ready to implement action plans. One way of helping clients feel more at ease with a new idea is to allow them to become accustomed to the 'feel' or 'sense' of it. Doing a 'Guided fantasy' exercise can be helpful.

Guided fantasy

This face-to-face exercise asks the client to live the new idea in their imagination. Box 6.9 has a suggested text for such a fantasy. The exercise requires confidence and familiarity with the use of 'guided fantasy' techniques (see Whitmore, 1990).

Box 6.9 Text for guided fantasy

Begin with a short relaxation exercise. The following instructions should be read out slowly with gaps of 15–30 seconds between each sentence:

Now you feel relaxed, I would like you to picture yourself in five years' time. You feel very content with your life. You are working in […], your chosen occupation. I'd like you to imagine a typical day. You get up, really looking forward to your day. You get dressed – what are you wearing? You have breakfast and go to work – how do you get there? Are you alone or is there someone with you? You arrive at work – take a look around you before you start work. What does it look like? Are there any other people present? What are you particularly looking forward to about your day? You start your work – how do you spend your morning? [And so on.]

When they have reached the end of the day, clients can be asked to write down their fantasy.

Such an exercise can produce new ideas, rather than just flesh out an existing one. It can also give rise to strong feelings:

> When she came to her final meeting, Geraldine's muddled feelings were still evident. It seemed there was some major block to moving forward, but neither she nor the counsellor knew what that was.
>
> A guided fantasy produced two major results. First, a brand new work idea evolved, which drew on some of the (previously muddled) earlier ideas. It seemed a practical one. In addition, the discussion after the fantasy revealed the crucial block to moving forward – the confusion Geraldine felt about her desires for a child and her ambitions for career success. This discussion released Geraldine's energy, which enabled her to formulate an action plan covering both work and non-work objectives. A further meeting was arranged to review the plan after three months.

Positive self-talk

Through the counselling, clients may feel encouraged to think more positively about possibilities. But negative self-talk may still prevail (see pp. 69–70). Some examples of the negative thinking which tends to occur when considering action are:

- I'll never be able to do it.
- I always fail at anything new.
- I mustn't make a fool of myself.
- I'm too stupid.
- It won't work.
- Others will disapprove.
- I'll feel angry, resentful or full of self-pity (and I couldn't bear that, I'd go to pieces).

The career counselling process itself may have the effect of reinforcing a client's decision, and thus counter some of these self-defeating beliefs. It may also be useful to encourage clients to talk to themselves more positively by asking:

- What's the worst thing that could happen?

Or to get them to say:

- I may feel stupid, but it's not the end of the world.
- I can only try my best.
- The choice may not be perfect, but that's OK.

It is helpful to ask clients to write down their negative thoughts, and then convert each thought into a more assertive and determined form of words. Box 6.10 gives some examples.

Box 6.10 Encouraging positive self-talk

It's difficult for me to …	It's a challenge to …
I'll try to …	I'm going to …
I can't … because	I could … if …
I wish that …	I know that …
I should … but …	I will …
I don't want …	I do want …

Positive self-talk can help clients to reduce their feelings of compulsion about success and failure, and increase their ability to cope with disappointments after the counselling has ended. Yost and Corbishley (1987) discuss additional techniques for helping clients who are experiencing difficulties in making career decisions.

Endings

The end of the relationship between client and counsellor in career counselling may be less of an issue than the end of the counselling relationship in some types of personal counselling, for the following reasons:

- Career counselling is usually a short-term process. The client comes for career counselling because of a particular career issue which may require a decision or action within a relatively short period.
- The contract establishes that the meetings are a structured support to the client's own thinking and working through of the career issues brought.
- Dependency is never encouraged within the counsellor–client relationship.
- A series of meetings is arranged, so the end is in sight from the beginning.
- The action plan is not the end of the career counselling process. The final meeting can be used as a way of reviewing progress, tackling any stumbling blocks, revitalising flagging motivation and celebrating successes.

It could be argued that, if a client were to feel bereft at the end of career counselling, the career counsellor would not have done a very good job of enabling and facilitating the client. However, like the mountain guide who takes the travellers to the pass, and then leaves them to ascend to the summit alone but well equipped to undertake the remainder of the journey, at the end of the final meeting the career counsellor says 'goodbye', leaving clients equipped with the skills and confidence to pursue their action plans independently.

Anne wanted career counselling to help her assess her capabilities. She 'fell into' teaching but had never felt happy in it. She also wanted to clarify why she had found it so difficult to thrive in teaching, and find an appropriate alternative career.

(Continued)

(Continued)

By the penultimate meeting, Anne had identified some clear work preferences: 'I like working at my own pace, with a varied work schedule. I like to work on my own, but with access to people at regular intervals. I enjoy putting things in order, interpreting numbers, working systematically and getting an end-product.' In this meeting, Anne discussed how these preferences related to different kinds of career and work environment, and talked over her feeling of panic about the possibility of a change.

She decided to hand in her notice and to research alternative occupations. Becoming an accountancy technician particularly appealed to her eye for detail and order. She left the career counselling room with a sense of release from the past, and new energy for the future.

However, not all endings are so neat and tidy! Some clients will still experience feelings of loss about saying goodbye, particularly if they have had some difficult endings in their lives. It may be appropriate, at times, to provide a few extra meetings to support a client through a hard time.

Laura's husband had recently died of a heart attack. They had been married for ten years. Her mother had died of cancer two years previously. Although she had had some bereavement counselling which had been a great help, her social life had revolved around her husband and his work. The rapport between Laura and the career counsellor was strong. The career counsellor avoided a potential trap by acknowledging Laura's need for a friend, and by helping her to reconstruct a social life and develop friendships. On the career front, she decided to study for A-levels and apply to university. Although she had met her career counselling objectives after four meetings, she was not ready to say 'goodbye' to yet another person, and she decided to arrange three more meetings with the career counsellor, spread over the next year.

Final meetings, too, are not always the place to tie up every loose end. Counselling skills must always be appropriate, and some final meetings may be completely taken up with working on emotional issues:

Barry's emotions required a lot of attention in his final meeting. He was not ready to move on and make a decision. With a trip abroad planned, and no fixed home in this country, he was not able to leave behind his career as a dentist. Counselling had, however, enabled him to face some important issues in relation to his life and career, and had increased his resolve to sort out his life in general before making a career decision. It would have been a pointless exercise at this stage to get him to complete an action plan.

(Continued)

(Continued)

The counsellor asked Barry to write with a report on his feelings and thoughts following the counselling. In his letter, Barry was able to acknowledge that he was 'lacking any interest to follow dentistry'. There was also a glimmer of energy emerging towards a new direction: 'I've taken some limited action about starting my own business – I've written to ... and spoken to ... .' He admitted his fears and needs: 'I'm very scared to get financially involved and perhaps lose everything. I need more security, especially at the moment.' He was able to analyse his 'stuckness': 'I just don't seem to be able to think about such a thing – I guess that's why I'm firmly stuck in the dentistry rut and "afraid" to get out of it.'

The final meeting had focused on Barry's blocks, and the possibility of psychotherapy was discussed. The career counsellor had recommended appropriate reading, and Barry confirmed in the letter his desire to pursue some kind of self-awareness activity. 'I am prepared to give it a try on my own, but feel I may need some help in getting going.'

The ending was not clear-cut. Career counselling brought to the surface some potent issues and feelings for Barry. Not only must career counsellors be aware of and skilled in dealing with this possibility (see Chapter 8 for further discussion), they should also be aware that a client may blame the counsellor for any newly surfaced negative feelings, as Barry's letter shows:

'I feel very confused ... almost angry and rather disillusioned with career counselling.'

But he was able to accept some responsibility in this process:

'I don't feel I have been given a very clear direction, but that's probably my fault, not yours.'

Of course, the self-defeating patterns evident in this letter match the still unresolved patterns emerging in the counselling, that is, the 'blame vs. self-blame' and 'should vs. want'. But Barry still wished to continue the career counselling process with the counsellor:

'I would like to meet you again ... and discuss things further – hopefully, by then, I'll be feeling a lot more positive about myself and my career direction.'

Continued support

People vary greatly in their need for support, but access to someone with whom they can talk over their plans and their progress is important for most clients. People need to be able to discuss the results (good or bad) of the action they have taken. Most find it helpful to have someone on their side, who believes in them and respects them, even if they are rejected. It is also encouraging to have someone to recognise and praise even small successes and achievements, and in due course to help in celebrating the completion of the action plan. Box 6.11 indicates some of the functions of review meetings:

Box 6.11 Some functions of review meetings

- Recognise small successes
- Celebrate achievement of action plan
- Re-focus action plan
- Tackle setbacks and current challenges
- Review overall strategy
- Discuss progress of research
- Rehearse job search approaches (e.g. preparing speculative letters, networking, CV preparation, interviews)
- Counselling for unresolved personal issues inhibiting progress (for example, continuing negative feelings about a recent redundancy or managing an unsupportive work context)
- Addressing a persistent self-limiting belief (see pp. 69–70)
- Coaching for a specific work-related issue (e.g. time management)

We build a review meeting into the career counselling programme. Without it 'built in', many clients will not take the initiative to make an appointment. Once this meeting is complete, most clients still appreciate the offer of further support in the future, should this be necessary. The majority of clients will probably not need to take up the offer, but the career counsellor should be clear about what any offer of support encompasses. It is helpful to consider the questions in Box 6.12.

Box 6.12 Offering support

- Are you offering further meetings to the client? For what purpose? How many? How often?
- Are you offering telephone contact to the client? For what purpose? How long? How often?
- Are you offering contact by letter to the client? For what purpose? On what basis?
- Are you offering other services to the client, for example help with CV preparation, interview practice, writing a reference? On what basis?
- If fees are involved, be clear about what fee is payable and what is not.

Recontracting for further meetings beyond the career counselling contract agreed may be a possibility, so long as the career counsellor has the appropriate skills, training and supervisory support.

Techniques to maintain momentum

By the end of the action-planning stage, clients often feel in a position to move forward. Some will have made quite dramatic progress; they may see their goal in sharp focus, and feel optimistic and energised. The tasks in the action plan will probably be at the forefront of the client's mind. Clients will often remark at this point 'It's all down to me now. I know what I have to do, and only I can do it.'

However, there is a danger that, on leaving the career counselling room, clients may slump back into old patterns, which often involve procrastination and delaying tactics. With the best will in the world, good intentions may fade, and competing demands may act to ensure that the action plan gradually goes further and further down the client's mental 'in-tray'. This problem of inertia should be anticipated. A number of techniques may be used to try to facilitate the career development process after the initial contract between client and career counsellor has been concluded, and to encourage and support clients in putting their action plan into practice. The techniques are all variations on the theme that, while it is easy to ignore one's own good intentions, it is more difficult to ignore external reminders – people or things that the client cannot put to one side so easily.

Rehearsal

While effective career counselling can help some clients to articulate their desired direction more clearly, others may need more help to 'rehearse' job interviews, networking and speculative approaches. Rehearsal can be especially beneficial for clients lacking the confidence to present themselves in a competitive and unfamiliar environment. Women 'returners' and others who have not applied for jobs for many years will be particularly affected (see Chapter 8, p. 134).

Use of a summary

Shortly after the final meeting, the career counsellor can send a summary to the client. This can be a three- or four-page document which sums up the client's progress during the career counselling and what he or she needs to do next. It may contain the key points arising from the exercises, tests and meetings, together with the action plan. Such a summary acts as an external record of the career counselling process, and for some clients it provides a psychological link with it. Receiving the summary can sometimes fuel the process of taking action. (Incidentally, writing the summary is a useful rounding-off and letting-go process for the career counsellor too – see Chapter 8.)

An alternative, or additional, approach is to invite clients to write their own summary. For some clients, this could be a practical way to remind themselves of the key points, take ownership towards acting on the career counselling, and draw a line under the career counselling relationship – 'That's over now; I'm on to the next stage.'

Other physical reminders

Just pinning the action plan up somewhere visible can be a helpful reminder. Clients often spontaneously think of their own devices for prodding themselves into action. Getting organised by setting up a special work space (even if it is just a 'Career development' box file) can be useful. Some clients start a career development diary or use a wall-planner to record their progress. Others timetable a 'career review' meeting in their diary. Clients can be asked to write a letter to themselves outlining their goals and plans and send it to the counsellor. The counsellor then posts it back to the client after an agreed interval (for example, in three months' time) to act as a reminder.

Support from others

Clients can be asked to think of one or two people on whom they can rely for wholehearted support in putting their action plan into practice. Likely people might include a partner, friend, colleague, sister or brother. Clients are encouraged to discuss their action plan with their supporter, and to arrange regular support meetings.

Rewards

As many counselling textbooks recommend (for example, Egan, 2002), it is helpful if clients can be encouraged to build in rewards for taking various steps to fulfil their action plan. For example, after completing an application form, a client might reap the reward of reading a chapter of an enjoyable novel.

Summary

This chapter has described several techniques for assisting clients with decision making, defining career goals and planning action. Although this can be a straightforward process, clients' anxieties may be raised as they approach a decision point, so the need for the career counsellor to respond to clients' emotions right until the end has been emphasised. Different ways in which the career counselling may end have been illustrated, and various means of encouraging clients to maintain momentum after the relationship has finished have also been discussed.

Chapter 7 looks at the role of career counselling within organisations, the content of such discussions and the dilemmas facing those offering such support.

Checklist: Action, outcomes and endings

☑ Clients can be better prepared for the 'ending' of the career counselling by including clear objectives (that is, ending criteria) in the contract.
☑ Expect that some clients will show 'resistance' towards the end of the career counselling; this could come from a fear of change.

(Continued)

(Continued)

☑ Encourage clients to acknowledge, and thus make overt, any progress made during the career counselling.

☑ Some clients will benefit from setting SMART goals *before* deciding on action (the 'what?' before the 'how?').

☑ Encouraging positive self-talk in clients may increase their ability to cope with setbacks.

☑ Consider building in a 'review meeting' into the career counselling contract.

☑ Be open to 're-contracting' with clients, so long as you have the necessary skills.

☑ Be clear about the terms of any further contract.

☑ Remember that not all endings are neat and tidy!

☑ Help clients with tangible techniques to maintain momentum.

7 Career Counselling in Organisations

Career support of different kinds has been available in a few organisations for many years. This chapter begins with a discussion of why so many more employers now recognise career counselling as a useful tool to enable their staff to address career issues. Then we discuss the ways career counselling is being used in organisations – what is discussed, who provides it and what the outcomes are. Because of the differing perspectives on the benefits of career counselling – how much it is to the benefit of the individual or the organisation, or indeed both – we then look at a number of dilemmas that people offering career support within, or for, organisations may experience. These focus predominantly on the effective management of boundaries and the need for clear contracting and screening, as described in Chapter 3. Finally, we pose a few questions for anyone considering beginning, or developing, career-support services.

Why the need for career counselling in organisations has arisen

Over the past ten years, employers have significantly reduced the numbers of people they employ: this has been market-driven, influenced by narrower profit margins, increased competition from local and global markets, more sophisticated IT-driven systems and the outsourcing of services previously offered in-house. These pared-down organisations, lean almost to the bone of any excess resources, have to get the very best out of their existing staff, as well as keep their most valued people.

In a competitive marketplace, where market value is influenced by public and shareholder confidence, 'managing reputation' is also seen as key, as employers seek to enable staff to leave their employ with what one manager called a 'healthy goodbye'.

Employers have also encouraged more 'self-managed' career development, implying that employees are expected to think and act for themselves in planning their career futures. Perhaps because annual employee surveys often reveal that staff think their organisation is doing too little to help them in this endeavour, employers are now responding by offering appropriate resources, including learning and development advice and career support. This may be a knee-jerk reaction to the criticism surfacing in employee surveys or part of a considered career-management programme.

Those staff most likely to leave when the job market becomes buoyant are those with the greatest confidence and market value. Research by Penna, Sanders and Sidney, an outplacement and career-management consultancy, entitled *Itchy Feet,* points out the 'ever readiness' of staff to move employer. Employees indicated that, faced with an environment of internal promotion (46 per cent), better training and development (41 per cent) and recognition of their work (36 per cent), they would, however, stay put. An effective career management strategy would include the following 'messages' to staff:

- We can't offer you a career for life – but we want you to progress your career for as long as you stay with us.
- We shall get to know our people very well, and try to make the best possible use of their abilities.
- We shall make sure that our employees understand the business, and the employment market, so they can have several realistic options in mind.
- We will make sideways moves accessible.
- We will help employees understand the relationships between the work and the skills required to do that work.
- We shall work with our employees as active partners in the management of their careers.

(adapted from Hirsch, 2002)

Such an approach can produce benefits of:

- increasing the commitment of individuals to stay and deliver;
- building the capability to meet future demands;
- becoming the 'employer of choice';
- reducing staff turnover, thus saving huge recruitment costs;
- enhancing 'competitive advantage'.

More broadly, UK government initiatives have encouraged lifelong learning, leadership development and a concern for managing mental and emotional wellbeing, including 'work–life balance'.

An example of an employer response to the work–life balance initiative is that of BT, which has introduced policies to encourage women to return to work after maternity leave, and to increase the time some staff can spend working from home.

Some large organisations, for example, Barclays Bank, have initiated major learning and development programmes. Barclays University was set up to offer state-of-the-art centres with excellent information resources.

Given then that employers need motivated, self-directed and productive employees who won't defect to a competitor, the existence of career support initiatives is now increasingly commonplace; this means that people in a wide variety of positions are seeking to develop career counselling skills.

The ways in which career counselling is being used in organisations

Employers offer a number of career-management support activities. These include:

- Career development workshops (for example, for those facing restructuring and possible job loss, as well as those considering career or job change).
- One-to-one counselling/coaching with an internal or external resource.

- Mentoring.
- Access to internal job market via Intranet.
- Career and self-analysis tools on Intranet.
- Succession planning.
- Outplacement support for employees leaving the organisation and wondering about their next steps.
- Career and personal-development workshops for potential senior managers, women, graduates and others at key decision points, and following attendance at a Development or Assessment Centre.
- External career workshops for senior managers wanting to review their career development to date, and plan the next phase.

For further discussion, see King (2004).

What is discussed in career counselling

Box 7.1 indicates some of the main areas talked about in career-support discussions.

Box 7.1 What do people talk about in career discussions?

- Where they are, feelings about work
- Skills and performance
- Values and drivers, work–life issues
- Potential and aspirations
- Options in the organisation and outside
- Processes and politics
- Pros and cons of choices – direction
- Next steps, whom to see
- Managing change
- How to network
- Stress and time management
- Re-integration after a secondment or placement
- Review following attendance at a Development or Assessment Centre
- Learning and development needs, and what is available.

See also Hirsch and Jackson (2004).

So who provides all this?

The above is a long list of topics, most of which require some expertise and knowledge, in addition to the skills of counselling, and the infrastructure to provide it.

Line managers play a key role in providing career support; a good deal is provided informally or semi-formally and sometimes by mentors. Hirsch and Jackson found that only 7 per cent provide career support in the annual review. They suggested that, whilst the line manager is a good starting point, they have limited information and power and should ideally be able to refer on.

In our experience, the following are involved in providing career counselling within, or for, employing organisations:

- Internal dedicated career counselling support service (for example, BBC, Shell) – provided for people wishing to assess the direction of their career, or to support people leaving the organisation.
- Trained pool of line managers across the organisation (for example, Audit Commission) – offering career discussions for staff at, and subsequent to, major organisational restructure.
- Learning and development specialists (for example, XL Capital Ltd) – linked to career development discussions with line managers.
- Training and development professionals (for example, Hillingdon NHS Trust) – linked to NHS 'Skill escalator' to encourage more flexibility to move jobs.
- Human resources and other development professionals (for example, BT) – as part of their work supporting 'talent development'.
- Mentors responsible for career support (for example, Ernst & Young) – for example, when considering partnership as a possibility.
- Internal counsellors and occupational psychologists (for example, PWC, Metropolitan Police) – support includes personal development, psychometric testing, development centres, coaching.
- External career counsellors (for example, Career Counselling Services) – career counselling programmes to 'take stock' of talents, skills, experience, values and motivation.
- Executive, performance and development coaches (for example, Ashridge Management College) – career counselling relevant when performance development is affected by lack of interest or poor talent fit.
- Outplacement services (for example, Executive Action) – career assessment and job search support for executives whose jobs are redundant.

What are the outcomes of career counselling?

Hirsh and Jackson reported the following examples of the impact of effective career conversations:

- future direction (reported by over 60 per cent of respondents);
- self-insight (60 per cent);
- values information (55 per cent);
- feel good (50 per cent);
- job move (37 per cent);
- career skills (22 per cent);
- retention (12 per cent).

Employers sometimes express the concern that, by providing career counselling, issues will be raised which may cause the individual to leave the organisation. Whilst this is an understandable fear, effective career counselling can lead to a 'win–win' outcome: it not only gives people the tools to enable them to do the very bidding employers want, that is, be 'self-directed' in their career management, but also respects the rights of individuals to be autonomous. Sometimes that means an individual will decide to leave the organisation, but that is relatively rare. If it does happen, it may well prevent the organisation from further months or even years of under-productivity. More likely, as the case of David shows, individuals will feel connected to their work, valued for their contribution, engaged with the organisation and motivated to contribute. Their willingness to apply and increase their capability will be enhanced. In turn, the organisation's capability to meet future demands will be enhanced by its ability to retain existing staff and to attract high-quality applicants, thereby unlocking the value chain which links personal success, business results and shareholder value.

> David is 34 and works for one of the top accountancy firms. He is regarded sufficiently well to be considered 'partnership' material. Of late, David has expressed doubt about his future in the organisation – he has long nurtured a wish to run his own business. He enjoys football coaching and refereeing at the weekends. He has also just become engaged.
>
> David is just not sure he wants the commitment that partnership will mean. His motivation has also gone right down, as he is overworked and has insufficient support, partly because several others in his department have left the organisation in recent months.
>
> His line manager, mentor and HR development adviser are agreed that some external, independent career counselling and 'assessment' may help him review his situation more objectively. They realise that they would be too biased to offer such assistance. They are concerned that, if they do not offer David some assistance, he will join the increasing numbers leaving the organisation. They agree that the content of the sessions will be confidential, and that David will report back afterwards with his reflections on the process and the results.

The following resulted from the career counselling:

> David's motivation for his current work increased – he became clearer that he enjoyed the management aspect of his work.
>
> He requested, and received, reassurance that he could work fewer hours, and have more support, in order to be freer to manage the work of others.
>
> He was still not convinced that he should develop to partnership level, but felt happier to 'go along' with things for now.

Although David's employers clearly had their own agenda, they were sufficiently realistic to allow him the autonomy to make up his own mind about his future. David's increase in motivation towards his current job is, in our experience, quite typical following employer-supported independent and confidential career counselling. Allowing him this autonomy demonstrated their respect for his opinion and right to make up his own mind.

Dilemmas for career counsellors working with organisation-sponsored clients

Many of the dilemmas faced by career counsellors working within, or for, organisations stem from the challenge of managing multi-agendas in relation to what end, and for whom, career support is provided. Consider the following perspectives of an individual seeking career counselling, and the employer who provides it:

Individual's perspective of potential gains from career counselling:

- I need feedback on my strengths.
- I want to use it to leverage my next career move.
- I need and want a sense of direction.
- I can use it to gain some skills for managing my career.
- I want to talk to someone who is neutral.

Employer's perspective of potential gains from career counselling:

- We can manage, and possibly improve, performance.
- We can use it for succession planning.
- We can identify potential.
- We can provide it for people leaving the organisation.

There is plenty of potential for the alignment of objectives between employer and individual, but these few examples imply the need for absolute clarity about what is on offer, who is offering it, and what will be done with any outcomes. Box 7.2 lists the typical dilemmas likely to be encountered.

Box 7.2 Typical dilemmas when offering career counselling within organisations

- Who is the 'client'? Are you working for the benefit of the organisation or the individual? Can you benefit both? How can you guarantee confidentiality?
- How do you manage 'third-party' referrals? Does this affect your ability to be a dispassionate counsellor, or are you expected to cajole and persuade?
- How do you handle the sensitive issues of your own position of power, whilst showing respect for the client's autonomy?
- How do you handle 'follow-up' after the career counselling?
- Is your career counselling supported by a well-resourced infrastructure, such as a back-up of information and access to job and development opportunities?
- How do you respond to requests for career counselling 'high potential' staff or identified 'talent', when you believe that the career support should be available to all, particularly disadvantaged groups?

Who is the 'client'?

If the career counsellor is working independently of the organisation, the career counsellor is paid for by the employer, whose agenda may be quite different from that of the individual client. We have even heard talk of 'counselling someone out' of an organisation. Career counselling may also be provided as a 'sop' to a disgruntled, but needed, member of staff, without any implicit agreement to pursue the resulting actions.

In the case of David (see p. 113), both parties gained as a result of his increased motivation for the current job, and his determination to take the initiative henceforth in managing his career. Crucially, the career counselling led to a constructive dialogue between David, his line manager and HR support which, in turn, substantiated the career counselling discussions through jointly agreed actions. What underpinned the success of David's experience was an openly agreed contract between David, his employer and the career counsellor, a willingness to follow through the outcomes, and a respect for David's autonomy.

If the career counselling is offered within the organisation, it is again vital to communicate clearly what is being offered, the extent of confidentiality possible, to establish what are the employer's expected outcomes and to reveal whether the career counsellor has any other roles which may conflict with the career counselling.

Some examples of employer goals:

- Help employee choose the next step in the organisation (for example, whether to go for partnership).
- Gain a better understanding of what to do to increase the individual's motivation.
- Identify how best to make use of the individual's talents.

The employer's goals should therefore be identified and, once agreed, built into any contract. This will mean a prior discussion with the referring manager, which will also include agreeing the kind of feedback expected and thus the boundaries of confidentiality. Most of our employer sponsors are happy for the individual to feed back the results of the career counselling in a written summary and subsequent discussion, thus respecting the confidentiality between career counsellor and individual client.

Box 7.3 Managing the dilemma – checklist for 'Who is the client?'

- Have you shown respect for the rights and interests of all people with a legitimate interest in the outcome of any career counselling contract, without compromising any confidentiality agreement?
- Prior to beginning the career counselling, ensure that you clarify the career counselling contract. This should include the employer's expectations of outcomes, and clarity on any overlap with other areas which may impinge on the discussion, such as performance management.
- Become aware of all the interests and agendas in relation to the individual client; even if some agendas are conflicting, several may not be. In all instances, any other agendas will affect the agenda of the client before you, and therefore cannot be treated in isolation.

How do you manage third-party referrals?

Whether a referral is made for career counselling internally or externally, it is important to be fully aware of the expected outcomes of the person referring. Are the desired outcomes achievable without the referral? How well briefed is the person doing the referring about the nature of the career counselling on offer? Who would be the best person to give the career counselling?

It is desirable, but not always possible, to have complete transparency and agreement of the aims of any career counselling and what will happen with the 'output', as the following case of Bernard shows:

Bernard had been passed over for promotion, his management ability having recently been severely criticised. He had, however, refused to accept this adverse 'diagnosis' by his employer. They had reached a stalemate, and a referral for career counselling was suggested by a colleague in the same organisation, so that Bernard could gain an objective and independent view of his skills and potential.

Although the organisation had used the career counselling service over many years, this was the first referral by Bernard's manager. After the initial telephone contact, and a subsequent letter, it became clear that he expected a report to be written on Bernard after one interview! A subsequent telephone discussion led to an agreement which was clarified in writing. It was agreed that: (a) there would be four or five meetings; (b) there would be no feedback by the counsellor on the content of the discussions; and (c) following the career counselling Bernard would be expected to debrief his manager, but would have control over the content discussed.

In the first meeting, the confidentiality contract was restated to Bernard, who initially found it hard to trust. Through the establishment of a good rapport, however, Bernard was able to assess himself in a non-threatening atmosphere. By the end of the career counselling, he decided that he was more suited to an administrative, rather than a staff management, role. A few weeks later, a letter was received from Bernard's manager expressing how pleased he was with both the process and the outcome.

One reason why it is so important to insist on confidentiality is because of the danger that career counselling can be seen by the employer as a way of gathering external feedback to confirm a previously held view that, for example, the employee is not suited to a particular position. Sometimes, the career counsellor may feel pressure to collude with the employer to persuade the individual of a particular direction. In such a potentially threatening referral situation, it will be hard, if not impossible, to establish the trust necessary for open and effective career counselling.

Generally, employees who have been through career counselling are happy to share much, if not all, of the content with their employers, once any apparent threat has been removed and a positive plan agreed. In order to manage the reasonable requirement by employers for feedback, whilst maintaining the boundary of confidentiality, we encourage employer-sponsored clients to prepare a 'summary' of their career counselling and to report back to their employer those results relevant to the next step.

Geoff, an economics graduate seven years with the same employer, had begun to feel he was stagnating and becoming too pigeonholed and specialised. Following his career counselling, Geoff took charge of the feedback to his employer. As a result of writing his own report, and following subsequent discussions with his line manager and the human resources manager, he was able to leverage a significant career move within the organisation. His employer almost certainly avoided losing a valued and talented employee. They had gained a re-motivated member of staff, much clearer about his strengths, interests and career aspirations.

Box 7.4 Managing the dilemma – checklist for third-party referrals

- Have you agreed up-front the aims of the career counselling with the sponsoring manager, and how the 'outputs' will be fed back?
- Have you ensured that the person referring knows the nature of the services available?
- Could the issues raised be dealt with through means other than career counselling?
- Who is the person most likely to give objective and dispassionate career counselling?
- Have you agreed confidentiality, or any limitations to it, with both referrer and referee?
- Are all interested parties clear about how and to whom the outcomes of the career counselling will be communicated?

How do you handle the sensitive issues of your own position of power?

In any counselling relationship, where clients request help, they are making themselves vulnerable, thereby creating a power imbalance in the relationship. The power imbalance is exaggerated further where the person offering career counselling is operating in an organisation where that very power can be asserted to take away, undermine or enhance the client's livelihood, or is perceived to do so.

Career counselling is sometimes offered as part of a performance-management programme by human resource (HR) professionals. Whilst performance improvement is clearly an important goal, when it is combined with career counselling, individuals may not be sufficiently trusting of the person or the process to contribute to an open discussion, particularly when their performance is being called into question. On the other hand, they may reveal something about their career plans which could later be taken out of context, for example, if the HR practitioner also wears a 'resourcing' hat which involves advising line managers of the best people for future positions. This begs the question 'Who is the right person to be conducting the career counselling?'

The most safe and ethically sound way of dealing with this dilemma is to ensure that any career counselling is proffered only by people who do not have any responsibility for that individual's career development. It is also pragmatic, because the open conversations that are likely to ensue will lead to realistic outcomes, which the client will 'own' and thus be likely to drive forward. This approach also fits well into organisations espousing the value of 'self-directed' career management.

However, there any many HR professionals, as well as line managers, who are called upon to conduct career conversations with staff. It is not always possible to call upon either an external career counsellor or a colleague in the organisation who may be able to offer a more independent context. In these instances we would urge all those offering career conversations to read the checklist in Box 7.5.

Box 7.5 Managing the dilemma – checklist for sensitivity to power issues

- Have you considered the nature of the 'power dynamics' between you and the individual? How do you intend to manage them?
- Are you the right person to be offering this individual career counselling now? If not, who is?
- Are you aware that the individual may not be completely open?
- Have you ensured that the 'contract' with the individual is transparent, including the degree of confidentiality possible?
- Have you declared if there are any potentially conflicting interests at the outset, thereby giving the individual the autonomy to decide whether to buy into the career counselling part of the discussion, or to take it elsewhere?
- Have you made the individual aware of alternative sources of assistance, internally or externally?
- What have you done to ensure that the client is able to 'own' the outcomes of career counselling?
- Will you avoid using a client's remarks, made in confidence, out of context?

Dawn had been seeing her divisional HR representative for a few meetings now. She needed to talk to someone as she had become increasingly frustrated with her lack of progression in the organisation. She also thought that she might be able to influence her HR representative, as she knew he fed in information to some of the line managers who sat on the monthly 'career councils', which considered the career development of individuals identified as having potential. Although she thought she made her case well, she had also mentioned, in passing, that her husband was considering taking a position abroad.

In fact, he did not take up the position, partly because they were both hopeful of her gaining promotion. She was therefore quite shocked when, at their next meeting, her HR representative opened with 'And has your husband finalised his plans yet?'

How do you handle follow-up after the career counselling?

Unlike an independently positioned career counsellor, people offering in-house career support may play more than one role for the 'client', which can affect both the career counselling and the subsequent relationship. Also, both 'career counsellor' and 'client' will come across each other again in many different contexts, formal and informal, from meeting in the cafeteria, corridor or lift to participating in social events and even collaborating over a work project.

Because the boundaries are less obviously clear, they are easier to breach. Contact via email, being approached over lunch or formal requests for further meetings are all distinct possibilities. Additionally, there will be many opportunities for similar approaches from that individual's line manager, and other stakeholders.

Such possibilities necessitate the need for absolutely clear contracting. This needs to occur, as described in Chapter 3, at the outset. The 'terms of reference' should also have been communicated clearly in any written documentation describing the nature of the service offered, or in any written contract you agree with the individual (see Box 7.6).

Box 7.6 Sample career counselling agreement

This agreement is applicable during your programme of career counselling.

We will meet for …. meetings between [today's date] and ……… We can then review the need for further meetings. Our goals, agreed to day, are:

1 ....

2 ....

3 ....

Subsequent to the completion of our career counselling meetings, it is, of course, possible to have an additional discussion.

I will also send you a 'follow-up form' to complete some months after our meetings. That may also be a good time to think about the value of a further meeting.

Please sign below your agreement to the above. Thank you for your cooperation.

I agree to the above career counselling goals and format.

Signature ....

Formalising the terms of the career counselling relationship is important in all instances. Within an organisation, we believe it can help further to identify what is acceptable behaviour, and to distinguish what is 'in the box' and out of it. For example, formalising any follow-up meeting in this way is not only likely to cut down on casual, and possibly frustrating, approaches, but will also optimise the chances that good work can be done within the time allocated (see Box 7.7).

Box 7.7 Managing the dilemma – checklist for 'follow-up'

- Have you created a clear contract, preferably in writing?
- Have you taken steps to minimise the chances of casual and frustrating follow-up, by formalising how follow-up should be handled between you?
- Have you indicated clearly when the formal part of the career counselling is complete?

Is your career counselling supported by a well-resourced infrastructure – such as a back-up of information and access to job and development opportunities?

Hirsch (2003) addresses the features of effective career discussions. She cites the behaviours needed by those conducting career discussions. Counselling skills are important, but not all that is required. Giving information is also cited as a key skill. Ultimately, the perceived quality of any career discussion will depend on its output. This will include an action plan, supported by access to any relevant information. Such information could include:

- relevant websites and Intranet job search resources (for example, job vacancies online);
- names of people responsible for any identified areas;
- access to details of relevant internal or external development options (for example, courses in time/stress management, professional/technical development);
- information on trends and likely developments in the organisation, and any associated employment opportunities such as secondments and project placements;
- information on learning and development resources (where is the information stored?);
- introductions to your own contacts, where relevant; and
- referral resources for further support, internally or externally (for example, Employee Assistance Programme, Occupational Health, financial or legal advice).

It should also be made clear to your clients that they, too, have a responsibility for accessing information. In fact, it may be helpful to describe your role as a 'resource for resources', clarifying that clients are responsible for conducting their own research. It may also be advisable to include statements to this effect in your service's promotional information. Some services also include expectations of the role of the career counsellor and client in the initial contract (see p. 9). Box 7.8 provides a useful checklist.

Box 7.8 Managing the dilemma – checklist for information provision

- What kind of information will be of real use to my/our clients?
- Where is that information located?

(Continued)

(Continued)

- Is it available in accessible form?
- What should I tell clients is my responsibility, and theirs, in the identification and sourcing of information, including contacts?
- Do I have an adequate list of referral resources (of all kinds)?
- Am I clear how the informal sourcing of information works in this organisation (for example, networking)?

How do you respond to requests for career counselling 'high potential' staff or identified 'talent', when you believe that the career support should be available to all, particularly disadvantaged groups?

It is a fact that disadvantaged and minority groups, as well as those not deemed to be in the organisation's 'talent pool', are not given much in the way of career support. The reasoning goes something like this:

> We want to keep our talented staff – it's a competitive market out there. We need to let them know we are doing something for them, as well as get vital information about their potential and intentions.

In terms of 'cost–benefit', it clearly pays an employer to invest resources in those people it sees as future leaders or providing key technical know-how. Increases in salary motivate only up to a point. And, with flatter organisations, and consequently fewer promotional opportunities, talented people may well be attracted to other employers, unless they are sufficiently stretched, developed or believe that the organisation is investing in them.

The difficulty with this approach is that it does not respond to the 'systemic' nature of employee groups. For example, in the example of David (see p. 113), his problems arose partly because of increasing turnover in his own staff. One global pharmaceutical company put 10 per cent of its staff in one of the UK's largest pharmaceutical companies through a career development workshop. Research over two years showed that those who attended the workshop were half as likely to leave the organisation as those who did not (Jackson, 1990).

The example of Philip shows how the dialogue created in career counselling averted a poor, and probably mistaken, career decision.

Philip was 45, and had worked for a major UK bank for 15 years. He had recently split up from his wife, after 20 years of marriage. At work, he provided a key technical role in the business, having skills and knowledge at his fingertips that had taken years to acquire. Following a couple of thwarted attempts to gain promotion to a management position, Philip felt let down and quite angry. He threw his energies into developing his passion for things Italian – learning the language, cultural visits and more.

(Continued)

(Continued)

He approached the company's learning and development advice team to seek information about a business language course. During the meeting, Philip's anger towards the company came out. He seemed on the brink of leaving. The learning adviser saw that Philip's anger was driving his decision. His training told him that he should not encourage clients to 'act' when in the grip of strong emotions. So he encouraged Philip to return for a further meeting, and gave him a couple of questionnaires to act as a focus for discussing his interests and values.

It was during the next meeting that Philip revealed that his deepest anger was towards his ex-wife, rather than the company. The discussion about the questionnaires strengthened Philip's self-belief, and clarified how important were his 'technical/functional' needs.

Philip agreed to use the company's Employee Assistance Programme (EAP) to address his angry feelings further. He also committed to identifying ways of gaining further recognition for his technical expertise within the company, and set up an immediate meeting with his line manager.

This case reveals a number of reasons for providing professional career support for all staff who want it (see Box 7.9). Philip would not have featured on a list of 'high potentials', but his loss would have cost his employer dear. The company had also taken some responsibility for enabling an employee to avert a mistaken and potentially personally damaging career decision.

Box 7.9   Managing the dilemma – checklist for organisation-wide career support

- Accept that providing career support to 'high potential' staff is in the employer's interests.
- Remember there are many arenas within the organisation where career discussions can take place (for example, learning and development discussions, performance management, coaching and feedback). An informal chat may alert the individual to the availability of support services.
- Consider making the business case for broadening career support, by presenting practice and results in other organisations (see King, 2004).
- Encourage individuals to seek career support themselves; this may be organised 'locally', without it necessarily becoming organisation-wide.

Making the case for more systematic and professional career support

If your organisation has yet to introduce effective career support, you will need to consider a number of key questions:

- *What is on offer already, and is it working?*   Track what career conversations go on now, whom do people approach, what works and which resources you can draw on. Can staff approach others in the organisation to talk about career issues without their line manager getting cross?
- *To whom would you initially offer career support?*   Be wary of positioning career support as a 'crisis only' service, unless you are happy for it to serve solely the needs of staff in a crisis situation.
- *Where are the most fruitful career discussions likely to occur?*   Career conversations can be:

  - formal or informal, structured and 'diaried' or available 'on the hoof';
  - one to one or career planning workshops;
  - via training and development events;
  - offered internally through line managers or HR and development professionals;
  - referred to external career counsellors, especially when an internally driven conversation is likely to be overly influenced by conflicting agendas, when relationships are not conducive to an objective discussion or when an external view may well add value to internal perspectives.

- *Do staff know they can come and talk to someone in Human Resources and Development about their career?*   You will need to address how you communicate what is on offer.
- *Do you have people trained in career counselling?*   Training is essential for every manager offering career support. See Appendix E for details of providers of career counselling training.
- *What would be the business benefits of investing in career counselling?*   Think of the 'bottom line'. You need to justify any investment. For example, the Audit Commission justified training a pool of line managers across the organisation during a time of significant change and upheaval, as it not only saved expensive one-off outplacement fees, but also built into the desired culture of continuing development for all staff.
- *How would career counselling tie in with related activities, such as performance management, succession planning, assessment procedures and recruitment processes?*   Career-planning activities should be driven by individual requirements, and should feed into the organisation's career-management activities, along with, but separate from, performance management, succession planning, assessment and recruitment. Mix them up, and you will find it hard to do one of them successfully; 'short-termism' will prevail, with career planning, being a longer-term activity, losing out.
- *What information and other resources do you, or could you, offer on the Intranet?*   Ensure that you combine any online self-assessment exercises with opportunities to talk these through with someone trained in career counselling. Provide accurate and up-to-date information, but neither overload people nor use the Intranet instead of face-to-face career support; they should complement each other.
- *What is the organisation's strategy on career management, and how well communicated, understood and practised is it?*   If you are not clear what the strategy is, write a draft, and get it firmed up with the top person responsible before implementing any processes. The clearer you and your colleagues are, the easier it will be to communicate the services clearly.
- *Are staff asking for better career management support through the employee survey?*   We often see career support services initiated following negative comments in the annual staff survey. It is important that there is a balance of responsibility in driving careers forward, shared between the employer and employee. Ask yourself not just 'Are we doing enough?', but also 'Are they doing enough?'

The next chapter addresses a number of professional challenges and questions that the career counsellor will typically face in practice, and outlines some of the specialist knowledge required.

Checklist: Career counselling in organisations

☑ Remember that an effective career-management strategy, and career counselling and other measures to support it, can contribute significantly to valued staff staying in the organisation.

☑ Ensure that, as far as possible, any career support is offered confidentially and is separated from other roles, such as recruitment and resourcing.

☑ Remember that informal career conversations can be just as effective as those conducted formally.

☑ Agree the aims of any career counselling with the referring line manager, and how any 'outputs' will be delivered.

☑ Ensure that good quality information is available and accessible following career counselling.

☑ Have a clear strategy on career management to inform the kind of practices and support needed.

---

8 Professional Challenges for Career Counsellors

Many issues that arise in the practice of career counselling have already been raised in previous chapters. Here we will take a closer look at some of those challenges and dilemmas most commonly arising for career counsellors. These include:

- managing the boundaries between career counselling, personal counselling and coaching;
- referring for further or alternative support;
- responding to the pressure to give advice;
- dealing with client resistance;
- working with 'significant others'; and
- working effectively with clients from 'minority' groups in a way that respects differences but does not reinforce stereotypes.

In Chapter 7 we addressed some key dilemmas for people conducting career counselling in organisational settings. Later in this chapter we will sum up the particular kinds of skills and knowledge required for career counselling.

Key professional challenges for career counsellors

Does the client need career or personal counselling?

Clients sometimes spend much of their first meeting discussing a personal issue. Apparently, if friends, colleagues and family enquire about a client's visit to a *career* counsellor, it is more socially acceptable than seeing a *personal* counsellor.

In addition, some clients come for *career* counselling consciously expecting to discuss their career, but actually use the time, sometimes to their own surprise, to discuss personal concerns. The dilemma for the career counsellor concerns the degree to which personal issues are allowed to dominate the sessions. On the one hand, career counsellors need to allow clients to acknowledge and, where appropriate and relevant, to explore their feelings. If, however, the career counsellor allows the client to pursue the personal route at the expense of the career issues originally identified, it is possible at the end of the meeting that a client will say or think 'I didn't get what I came for.'

At some point, therefore, it may be appropriate to remind a client of the *career* nature of the contract. If the personal issues prove persistently dominant, it could be helpful to renegotiate the contract or discuss the possibility of a referral elsewhere (see also Chapter 3). Box 8.1 suggests some questions which may enable the practitioner to decide whether career or personal counselling is more appropriate.

Box 8.1 Some questions to clarify whether career counselling is appropriate

- Is the emotion that a client feels about a problem so debilitating that it must be looked at first?
- Does this client have sufficient 'attention' to deal with the career issue/choice?
- Is the career issue the least of the client's problems?
- Is the client being unreasonably demanding of the career counselling process?

The emotion a client feels about an event like redundancy is often so debilitating that it must be looked at first, as in the following case:

> Timothy (see p. 27) had recently been made redundant, after 25 years with the same employer. He had no friends and few hobbies outside his work, and had devoted himself to work achievements, often staying well past the required time. He was not only devastated by the news of his redundancy, but was also virtually incapacitated by the anxiety he subsequently felt. In the first meeting with his counsellor, it emerged that Timothy had 'used' his work to avoid facing some earlier painful experiences.

Timothy's painful childhood needed to be addressed, or at least acknowledged, before he could make a rational consideration of his future, and prepare himself for anything like an effective job-hunting effort.

The reality of being out of work introduces another dilemma. The client's need to meet basic expenditures, let alone earn a decent living, does not go away. Counselling can take a length of time inconsistent with the client's sense of urgency to get a job. One expedient solution might be to give some time to the personal issue whilst the client is taking advantage of all available state benefits and becomes aware of, and possibly participates in, government-sponsored training or retraining programmes. This may reduce the client's sense of urgency whilst allowing time to work on the underlying problem.

The most appropriate way forward will depend on many factors, such as the intensity of the client's reaction to the redundancy, the expectation of re-employment, and the client's own emotional and financial supports.

Sometimes the career issue seems to be the least of a client's problems, as in Joanna's case:

> Joanna was 46 and had a reasonably successful career as a features journalist. She had even been able to combine this work with her interest in health and complementary medicine. However, since her husband had left her two years earlier, she had experienced periods of deep depression, along with a strong desire to 'find
>
> *(Continued)*

(Continued)

herself'. Stripped of both a partner and the prospect of motherhood, her grief needed further time and support before she could resolve her career dilemma, which she saw as a choice between developing her fictional writing and a complete change of career. Her concern to get on with her life alerted the counsellor to the possibility that she had not only insufficiently worked through her grief, but was also denying it. The counsellor felt that unless Joanna recognised what was happening to her she would continue to be blocked about her career, and suggested a referral to a bereavement counsellor.

Joanna's career dilemma was only the 'presenting problem', and, although its resolution was a priority, one career counselling meeting brought out more underlying issues which needed attention first.

Other situations appropriate for referral

As indicated above, the need for referral may arise at any stage in the career counselling. Having completed the counselling, a referral may still be appropriate if, for example:

- career counselling has raised the client's awareness of the need for personal counselling about a major life issue from the past; or
- the client needs specific information which the career counsellor cannot provide (for example, about particular occupations, or educational grants/loans).

The career counsellor needs a bank of referral resources: names, addresses and telephone numbers of local advisory bureaux and nationwide directories of counselling and psychotherapy services. One useful publication, annually updated, is the British Association for Counselling and Psychotherapy's *Counselling and Psychotherapy Resources Directory*, available online and in hard copy. It is particularly useful to build up a list of counsellors and other support services which can be personally recommended.

Any referral should be made with care, especially referrals for personal counselling. Such a suggestion can easily be interpreted by the client as a rejection, and may interfere with the rapport ('You think I'm crazy' or 'Someone else can't help me – I've failed again'). The career counsellor, of course, needs to be prepared to deal with the client's feelings during any discussion about referral. For a referral to be successful, the decision should be a joint one, and the reasons shared openly. It is quite reasonable, if appropriate, to suggest that the client can return for a further visit later on if it would be helpful. Making this offer can act as a useful 'bridge' for clients, even if they do not actually take it up.

In the case of 'referral' for specialist or detailed information about careers, it is useful to build up a list of personally known contacts in different occupations, who may act as 'human' sources of information for clients. This may be done by asking previous clients if they would be willing to be contacted. Addresses of professional associations should also be accessible. See Appendix C for sources of careers information.

Figure 8.1 **The overlapping functions of career counselling, development coaching and career coaching**

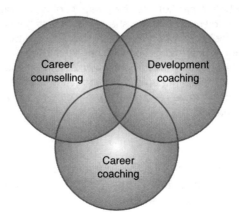

Does the client need career counselling or coaching?

This question is often raised by participants on career counselling training programmes. In recent years, coaching has become a buzzword, perhaps reflecting the more acceptable face of counselling as it implies, at face value, less of an emphasis on problems and more on goal setting and action.

We see career counselling, career coaching and *development* coaching as overlapping activities (see Figure 8.1). Development coaching enables people to develop their effectiveness in their current roles. This may lead to greater work satisfaction.

Career counselling focuses on the review of an individual's resources to make more informed choices. The realisation of those choices may be influenced by the person's ability to *develop* sufficient and appropriate skills, knowledge and attitudes. This could be facilitated by development coaching.

> Nick, 39, a solicitor in family law, was questioning his commitment to law as a profession. He disliked the emphasis placed on 'billing clients', and also felt that the politics of this small family-owned partnership excluded him from important knowledge and decisions. He had recently become engaged, and he and his fiancée were considering emigrating to New Zealand.
>
> It soon emerged that Nick's disenchantment was more with the way the firm was run than with the law itself. A need emerged for Nick to develop his assertiveness and time-management skills. The career counsellor, who had also been trained in coaching, recontracted with Nick so that the latter two sessions focused on Nick's coaching needs.

It is not uncommon for clients to approach a career counsellor when something has gone amiss with the immediate job or work environment. 'Is this the right career for me?' may be an acceptable 'entry point'. For some clients, that is indeed the right contract. For others, it may emerge after one or two sessions that, as with Nick, the way forward is more through development *within* this career choice, rather than precipitately moving out of it.

Career coaching overlaps both with career counselling and development coaching. We see career coaching as equipping clients to achieve their career goals by the effective use of career-management skills. These include:

- assertiveness skills;
- time-management skills;
- job applications;
- CV preparation;
- interview presentation;
- using the Internet;
- gaining information- and advice-seeking meetings;
- speculative approaches;
- networking.

Coaching a client in these career-management skills *does* require some 'technical' knowledge of what works. For example:

- What is 'assertiveness' and how can it be of use?
- What constitutes good time-management practice?
- What characterises a good CV?
- What *is* an information-seeking interview and how do you obtain one?

Career coaching will be most effective when it is combined with the use of core counselling skills and knowledge of the client. Although technical know-how will give the career coach credibility, it needs to make sense and work for the particular client.

Advice giving: the dangers

It is sometimes very tempting to give advice to clients in career counselling. After all, they often ask for it! However, we believe that, as a general rule, career counsellors should avoid giving advice, for the reasons given in Box 8.2.

Box 8.2 Disadvantages of advice giving in career counselling

- It absolves clients from taking responsibility for their own decision making.
- The advice may be wrong for this person.
- Decisions arrived at through personal reflection and experience are more likely to stick and be satisfying.
- If the advice is wrong, the counsellor is likely to be blamed.
- In giving advice, it is tempting to offer a pet like or suggest avoiding a pet hate.
- The inevitable challenges of a new job are likely to be more maturely managed if the original decision to move into that job is 'owned'.

Even occupational information should be given with care (see also Chapter 5), as the following example shows:

> It seemed very clear to the career counsellor that Jeremy's abilities, interests and personality indicated a certain group of occupations. Because of his training, he offered these suggestions merely as kite-fliers. However, the client avidly wrote them down.
>
> What the career counsellor had overlooked was that testing had established that Jeremy was someone who needed structure and liked working with facts. He therefore regarded the counsellor's suggestions and the information he gathered before the next meeting as absolute facts, not as ideas on which to reflect. When he read the occupational information, Jeremy became downhearted when he found that nothing he read seemed 'practical'.

Perhaps a more 'intuitive' client would have treated the career counsellor's ideas as they were intended – as ideas. But perhaps not. The combination of the client's need for a solution together with the perceived expertise of the counsellor is often so strong that almost anything suggested can be taken 'on board'. It is not uncommon to hear 'The counsellor said I should ...'. On the other hand, if the counsellor suggests 'Why don't you ...', some clients will use the opportunity to play the 'Yes, but ...' game (Berne, 1968).

Is it ever helpful to give advice?

Supposing the career counsellor feels convinced that the client is embarking on an inappropriate career choice. Does this constitute a case for intervention in order to save the client from what the counsellor thinks will be a dreadful mistake? Or even to protect those who will work with a client who subsequently might become embittered or even a danger? For example, an alcoholic who wants to become a firefighter, or a client who wants to become a counsellor, but is unwilling to deal with personal issues.

Some of the choices in this situation are:

- Say nothing (silence may, however, be read as agreement).
- Allow clients to see the pointlessness of the decision through experience, for example, by applying for training or employment and being turned down.
- Point out lists of the skills and personal qualities required.
- Suggest that clients put themselves in the position of employers recruiting for the desired occupation.
- Give a direct opinion.
- Conduct a 'Blocks and bridges' reality test exercise (see pp. 64–6). This confronts the client directly with the resources he or she has and lacks for that job choice.

A time when it may be appropriate to give advice is the stage when clients are relatively clear about their career direction and need 'technical' coaching on career-management and job-search techniques (see p. 129).

Client resistance

It can be very frustrating when clients:

- turn up late for appointments;
- miss appointments, usually giving a plausible excuse;
- fail to complete home assignments; or
- avoid keeping to the contract by, for example, continuing to expect the career counsellor to provide an 'answer'.

Such behaviour may be a covert expression of a client's feelings, particularly anger, and it may provide a useful 'message' about the client's problem, as in this case:

> Each time Roger was due to keep an appointment there was confusion. On one occasion, he telephoned to say that his car had broken down. He asked whether it was worth coming as he would be half an hour late. On another occasion, he forgot to attend at all.
>
> The 'truth' emerged when he was due to make a final appointment, and had to ask permission from his father, who was paying for the meetings.

In Roger's case, his father had wanted the career counselling to produce a particular result, and was only willing to finance the meetings if Roger used them in the way *he* wanted.

Although this is a relatively unusual example, some resistance or avoidance will tend to occur from time to time. The likelihood of such incidents and behaviour can be reduced by clear contracting. Where money is involved, payment at the first meeting for the whole programme, with a clear statement that missed appointments must be paid for, can test and increase commitment at the early stages of the career counselling. We find it useful to ask clients to sign a 'terms of business' contract, which highlights their responsibility to turn up for appointments, and on time. Whether or not the client is paying, the contract also lays financial responsibility for missed appointments with the individual client. However, resistance cannot be eliminated and career counsellors might use such signs as a basis for:

- questioning the client's commitment to the career counselling;
- exploring who else has a vested interest in the outcome of the career counselling;
- challenging clients to make their covert anger more overt (and therefore less likely to be acted out in the client–counsellor relationship);
- considering whether career counselling is not meeting the client's real needs;
- giving adequate time to acknowledging how the client is feeling; and
- questioning the client's commitment to 'work' (perhaps as defined by a significant 'other').

Working with 'significant others'

Although the career counsellor is always responsible to the individual client, there will be occasions when another party is involved in, or will be affected by, the client's decision-making process. This might be an employer (see Chapter 7), partner or parent.

In some cases, the client will have shared the tape recording made in an earlier meeting (see Chapter 5, pp. 81–2) with a parent or partner. Parents can be a big help to the career counselling process, because of their concern for and knowledge of their son or daughter. For the same reasons they can be a hindrance, frequently wishing to further their own agendas for their children, for example, by pressuring them to:

- follow the family line (for example, go to Cambridge);
- do the opposite of what they did (for example, don't run a business);
- take a particular course (for example, science or engineering, which is seen as vocational and more likely to lead to a secure job); or
- not to waste their time studying – 'it never got me anywhere'.

Joint meetings can air any conflicts between the young person and his or her parents, allowing their respective thoughts and feelings to be addressed in ways not done previously:

> Alan and his mother were over half an hour early for the final meeting. When the career counsellor went into the waiting room, he found that Alan and his mum were already in the middle of a lively conversation about his career, and were addressing issues they had not done before.

On other occasions, however, it can be hard to avoid being pulled into the family 'system' and taking sides:

> The career counsellor was known to Emma, who had contacted the career counselling service with a view to sponsoring her nephew Jamie. In the first meeting with Jamie, it became apparent that he had resolved to follow a particular career, and wanted to use the time to explore ways in which he could build on his strengths and minimise the impact of his weaknesses within his chosen career. However, in the final meeting, Emma wanted to know why the career counselling had not assessed Jamie's suitability for different careers. She was convinced that his choice of occupation was utterly wrong.
>
> The career counsellor felt pulled in different directions but attempted to enable Emma and Jamie to hear each other's points of view. This was virtually in the form of 'interpretations' and mediating what one was saying to or about the other.

Third parties can also become involved in the career counselling indirectly. One example was a married man who was 'encouraged' by his wife to come. It proved productive to look at his feelings about her desires for his career as part of the process of considering what career might be appropriate for him. Another example was a man of 24 whose father paid for the career counselling, and was disappointed that the counsellor had not recommended a career more in line with his own expectations. In fact, the client had seemed happy with the outcome of the work, but, because the career counsellor had not taken sufficient account of the influence of the father over his son, the apparently good result was undermined.

Even more indirectly, significant third parties can be involved in the career counselling without even being present in the room. They may be partners, parents or employers, whose 'presence' seems to dominate the client's thinking. This can be particularly true at the initial contracting stage when the career counsellor is building the relationship with the client, and wanting to establish that the client is truly engaged and committed to the career counselling (see Chapter 3).

For a discussion of issues arsing from employer-sponsored clients, see Chapter 7, 'Career Counselling in Organisations'.

Working with clients from 'minority' backgrounds

As we mentioned in Chapter 2, factors such as race, class, gender and disability are important in determining an individual's career development, and career counsellors need to have an understanding of diversity issues in order to practise career counselling in a way which counters the effects of oppression on people from 'minority' groups.

Ideas, attitudes and assumptions about people who do not conform to the 'norm' of the 'majority' culture can operate against the interests of people from certain groups, so that they have unequal life chances. They do not have equal access to educational and employment opportunities. They face an extra task of coming to terms with what the issue of being black, female or working class means in terms of barriers and obstacles to their career development, as the following case study shows:

> Chris was 27 and approached a career counsellor to discuss his future prospects. He was born and educated in Britain but his parents had emigrated from the Caribbean. His school encouraged him to achieve on the sports field but not academically. He left with only two GCSEs, but went on to study part-time at college whilst supporting himself financially through working as a fast-food assistant. He eventually achieved two good GNVQ passes and tried for a better job. After many unsuccessful attempts to get an office job, he decided to apply for a business studies degree course. On graduating, he was unable to find a job in the commercial sector, but eventually found work as a clerical assistant with the local council. After two years, he was promoted to a supervisory role. Still trying to better himself, he had meanwhile begun to study for a postgraduate management qualification in his own time. He had not told his manager about his studies, and had just been sent on a low-level supervisory training course.

In the career counselling it emerged that, understandably, Chris was diffident about 'blowing his own trumpet' regarding his management studies, for fear that his expertise would yet again be rejected. It was important for the career counsellor to validate Chris's feelings of frustration at all the barriers he had encountered. However, the career counselling moved to a coaching level, helping Chris to develop his self-presentation and assertiveness skills. Later, Chris negotiated with his manager and was given projects which made use of the management skills he had acquired.

Here are a number of guidelines to enhance professional practice.

- Monitor how, for example, your own gender, cultural or racial background and social class affect your work with clients. Examine honestly your prejudices and conditioning. Stereotypes, for example, that Asians are good with figures or that gay men are effeminate, may prevent the unaware counsellor from seeing the individual objectively, and from listening and empathising effectively across class, race, gender, religion, age and any other boundaries.
- Accept that the anger and frustration that clients from groups which face discrimination feel is legitimate, and not due to an inner psychopathology.
- Be aware that if people are assailed from birth with messages that they are second class, their self-esteem may not be first class. Offer help such as confidence-building and assertiveness techniques to challenge discrimination, or refer the client to sources of such support.
- Remember that many people from minority groups will have experienced a disproportionate number of rejections when applying for jobs. In particular, it is likely that black clients will have encountered racism when dealing with predominantly white organisations, or will not even have applied to these organisations on the assumption that they won't be interested in 'people like me'. The reality is that many of these companies are now very interested in recruiting people from minority groups and have changed their style of advertising and their recruitment practices in order to do this.
- Encourage clients to examine the full spectrum of career options. Women may have been brainwashed into considering either the traditional 'wife and mother' role or a limited range of gender-stereotyped occupations. Black people may have less access to informal sources of occupational information in their own networks, and may need more help than white people in locating sources of information (see Chapter 5).
- When working with women, avoid perpetuating the 'having a career or a family' dichotomy. For some women who want children, the issue is no longer whether to do both, but how to do both. The debate about work–life balance has received such prominence over the last decade that most employers now have policies in place to address part-time and flexible working so that it is not an issue. Similarly, avoid the assumption that *all* women will want to do both.
- Whilst the issue of confidence may arise when working with anyone applying for a job, it *typically* arises with women, who tend to to apply for jobs only when they believe they can do most of what is required in the advertisement.
- Ensure that you properly understand and value qualifications that have been obtained elsewhere. In England, for example, one form that ethnocentrism (the belief in the supremacy of one's own culture) takes is assumptions and views that English qualifications are superior to qualifications gained elsewhere – in Nigeria, Ireland, Scotland, India, Jamaica or France, for instance.
- In the case of a client with limited written or spoken English, don't assume that this is evidence of limited ability. It is likely to be the consequence of a lack of relevant opportunities to learn English. Be aware that in a cross-cultural situation, both verbal and non-verbal communication may be more open to misinterpretation.

- Encourage women and people from minority groups to check out a potential employer's track record on career opportunities. Do they see 'different' people on the company website? Is there an espoused diversity policy? (There are plenty of organisations that are now successfully advancing people from traditionally under-represented groups.)

Skills and knowledge valuable to career counsellors

It is assumed throughout this book that all practising career counsellors will have developed, through a combination of training and experience, the core skills of counselling. Box 8.3 lists some of the skills, attitudes and behaviours that consti-tute the basis of all good counselling practice. The reader can discover more about these skills in Egan (2002).

However, in the practice of career counselling, a number of areas of specialist skill and knowledge are required in addition to these.

Box 8.3 Basic counselling skills, attitudes and behaviours

- Ensure that the physical setting is conducive to establishing trust.
- Make clear contracts with clients.
- Be clear about the boundaries of your own skills and role.
- Be aware of what interferes with effective listening.
- Respect clients and accept their social contexts.
- Use responding skills (including reflecting, clarifying, probing, summarising and open-question techniques) in an appropriate manner.
- Use challenging and confronting skills, where appropriate.
- Use silence appropriately.
- Be aware and have experience of at least one model of counselling.
- Be able to move clients on to the 'next stage' of the counselling from insight to motivation and action.
- Use techniques to set effective goals and action plans.
- Refer clients sensitively, as appropriate.
- Ensure that proper and adequate supervision is received.

Validating 'alternative' career patterns

Not only should career counsellors offer a *context* that is neutral and independent, they should be open-minded about the client's *relationship* to careers and work in general.

Some individuals seek a working lifestyle very different from the traditional pattern. They may want more flexibility to take 'time out' for training and develop-ment, or for travelling. They may also expect the flexibility to maintain a balanced work and personal life.

People who have followed a less traditional career pattern can no longer be seen by anyone, especially career counsellors, as failures. In addition to the vertical, upwardly mobile pattern of career development, there is the 'horizontal' pattern. As the name suggests, movement is across levels, rather than up the organisational hierarchy. For example, an industrial chemist, who does not want or is not seen by his or her employer as able to become a manager, may transfer to a new project. Or a systems analyst might move from a backroom analytical role to one involving more customer contact. Such development can be seen as a gradual process of learning, and is compatible with the demands of many large employing organisations today who need to have a staff able to adapt to their ever-changing requirements. It is quite likely that career counsellors will meet people who have jumped around from one occupation to another, without ever seeming to 'settle down'. They come for career counselling more confused by the disapproval of parents and the felt need for a consistent curriculum vitae, than by any sense of their own that they have failed or been in unsuitable work. Perhaps they see their lives more as a whole than in terms of occupational success alone. The work of the career counsellor may need first to focus on reaffirming such clients' sense of self-worth by validation of their 'cyclical' pattern of experience before planning for the future. There is, for example, a great deal of experience and skill that someone who has been a nurse, secretary, computer programmer, caterer and counsellor can offer, not least experience of many different organisational settings, styles of management and the skill of establishing relationships quickly.

For obvious reasons, the career patterns of women with children often appear more 'untidy' than those of men, and may involve a fresh start after child-rearing. It is important not to judge women's careers by male norms.

Career counsellors are also likely to see increasing numbers of 'older' workers, many of whom will too easily discount their experience and qualifications, thus seeing themselves as 'out of touch' and having low worth on the job market. The task of the career counsellor is to help these people see their *employability* by identifying not just transferable skills but also usable experience.

> Patrick had left school at 16, with few qualifications. His 'career' had seen a variety of businesses succeed and, latterly, fail. Now aged 55, he had high financial needs but a poor perception of his chances of finding work. He had never compiled a CV and his panic was causing him to apply for almost anything – a 'scattergun' approach which was lowering his morale further. The career counsellor helped Patrick to compile a detailed list of his life and work achievements, skills and contacts. This helped Patrick to see that he had a lot to contribute to those less experienced in business than himself. He subsequently found work as a small business adviser.

Patrick, therefore, could draw on his recent business failure and turn it to his advantage. Thus, virtually *any* experience can be drawn upon, and usually is. It's about convincing the individual that it is worth something.

Knowledge of alternatives to traditional full-time employment

In order to assist clients to develop occupational ideas, career counsellors should know about, or have access to knowledge of, alternatives to the conventional idea of a career. The reality is that fewer 'jobs for life' are available, and clients may still harbour hopes based on outmoded values and expectations.

By referring to the existence of alternative possibilities along with more conventional ideas, the career counsellor can validate as a viable alternative an idea which may be totally new to a client. Some possible alternatives to a full-time 'job for life', include part-time work, self-employment, franchising, cooperatives and temporary, contractual or freelance work.

The idea that a part-time position might allow time to develop a new skill can be very liberating for a client perhaps stuck in the belief that choices have to be made in the ways that they always were. Similarly, reducing from five to four days a week can allow a client to try out a business idea without full commitment.

The advantages of part-time work have now been recognised by both employers and individuals, and include:

- It gives paid experience (usable on a CV).
- It can provide a reference.
- It enables social contact to be continued.
- It can help to ease the change from full-time to self-employment.
- It provides continued activity and structure to the day.
- It may provide some of the finance required for part-time education or training.
- It may help to finance the setting up of a small business.
- It may lead to a full-time job.

Over the past ten years, the number of part-time employees in the UK has increased from one in five to one in four. Of the 7.3 million part-time employees, 5.7 million are women. Whilst a number of part-time jobs are low-paid 'outworkers', some employers are amenable to offering a reduction in working hours for their skilled professional staff.

Self-employment — a viable alternative?

Several clients will want to consider the possibility of some kind of self-employment, freelance or contract work. Career counsellors should be alert to the emotional challenges that clients face when leaving behind a relatively secure employment lifestyle to embrace the uncertainty of running a business.

Often, it is suggested that potential 'entrepreneurs' need to have particular characteristics, such as being a self-starter (see www.liraz.com/webquiz.htm). Others, such as S. and B. Hashemi (2002), suggest that many people dismiss the option of running a business because they have been led to believe that not just anybody can be an entrepreneur and that entrepreneurship is reserved only for superhuman visionaries. The reality is that running a business takes many forms: it could be a small service or craft-based business from home, or a franchisable growth opportunity such as Coffee Republic. Consequently, the qualities required will be very different.

At the very least, career counsellors should be able to put clients in touch with appropriate sources of help and advice (books, courses, agencies, banks and others). One idea to pave the way, and manage the potential risk, is to try something small whilst still in employment (for example, by reducing working hours) – to take a stepping stone.

'Stepping stones' – a technique of career development

Clients often come looking for the ideal job or career, partly as an antidote to their present confusion. The idealised version of their career will, they think, somehow remove all their misery. A useful point of focus for career counsellors is to be aware of clients' relationship with this ideal. It may be very important for the client to maintain it as an ideal: at least, the client believes, there is still something good that could be possible. But once the counsellor attempts to break down the dream idea into some realistic component parts, strong resistance may be shown by the client. The 'craft shop' in the country, the B&B or the café-bar idea may, however, provide the basis for developing a more workable and realistic proposition.

Once a more reasonable aim has been agreed, it is then possible to discuss with clients appropriate ways of getting there. Disappointing though it may be for clients, the next 'job' may not be *the* one. It is at this point that the career counsellor can introduce the idea of stepping stones as a legitimate and normal way of making progress towards an occupational goal. For example, the client considering starting a bed and breakfast establishment may decide to work for a while in a small hotel in the location under consideration. A social worker wanting to become a trainer may decide to teach social work for a couple of years, and take an appropriate qualification, before applying for training jobs. Someone wanting to enter the field of graduate recruitment may work first in a Connexions office, gaining knowledge and experience of working with young people.

Appraising clients of such possibilities can reduce their sense of urgency that the next job *must* be the right one. This applies equally to clients who feel they *must* leave their current employer, possibly because of a personality clash with a supervisor or colleague or because of disillusionment with their lack of progress. It may be possible to defuse a client's sense of urgency by describing the technique of stepping stones as a valid and viable way out of the organisation and, equally important, as an undoubtedly easier way of changing careers than approaching the job market directly. An example would be a salesperson who wants to move into marketing having a better chance on the open job market if he or she first gains marketing experience.

Social and cultural aspects of occupational choice and satisfaction

It is fashionable to talk of *transferable skills* – the helpful idea that skills may be transferred from one occupational environment to another (for example, teachers can take their 'persuading' skills to a sales career). However, there are factors other than the application of skills to tasks which contribute to occupational satisfaction and success. Of particular importance is the degree to which a person can adapt to the demands of an organisation's culture, that is, its values, expectations, systems of operation and reward, and its people. Some specific considerations include:

- size of organisation;
- private or public sector;
- centralised or decentralised control;
- security of employment provided;
- whether the organisation's espoused values match up to reality;
- flexibility of working hours and practices;
- formal or informal culture;
- opportunities for career and learning development;
- opportunities for gaining from success (for example, bonuses, dividends);
- nature of the product or service; and
- age and cultural make-up of co-employees.

Indeed, clients may sometimes be choosing organisational type, colleagues and a boss as much as the type of work (see also Chapter 5, pp. 85–8).

Awareness of the principles of self-managed career development

Career counsellors should be aware that many large organisations are encouraging staff to take charge of managing their careers, and that prospective employees will be expected to exhibit the same kind of 'pro-active' behaviour. This has implications for preparing clients to continue using the tools and techniques of career counselling once the sessions are finished.

In addition to continued self-assessment (hopefully a by-product of the career counselling), one important career-management skill is knowing ways of evaluating jobs and organisations (London and Stumpf, 1982). Arnold (1997) refers to the use of effective decision-making styles, which might be rational or intuitive; the key is that the style should suit the individual. Another is knowledge of an organisation's selection and recruitment practices, and the use of effective self-promotion techniques.

Summary

In this chapter we have considered some of the common challenges career counsellors may face in the course of their work. The questions addressed included:

- What are the boundaries between career counselling, coaching and personal counselling?
- When is referral appropriate?
- Is it ever appropriate to give advice?
- How can third parties affect the career counselling?
- How can career counsellors work best with people from certain minority groups?
- What are the particular skills, knowledge and other qualities required by career counsellors?

In the final chapter we look at self-management for the career counsellor.

Checklist: Professional challenges for career counsellors

☑ Be willing to allow clients to acknowledge their debilitating emotions.

☑ Offer flexibility between addressing clients' unresolved issues and their need to get a job.

☑ Be prepared to offer 'development coaching' when it may be a more appropriate strategy than career counselling.

☑ Use 'career coaching' when clients have established clear career goals.

☑ Work hard to gain clients' ownership of any decision. To that end, be aware of the dangers of advice giving.

☑ Use a 'terms of business' contract to highlight clients' responsibility to attend booked meetings.

☑ Be open to addressing the emotions that underlie clients' 'resistance' to the career counselling.

☑ Take into account how any 'significant others' may affect the process and outcomes of career counselling.

☑ Question your assumptions and prejudices with all clients, but especially when working with people having very different values, beliefs and life experience from your own.

☑ Ensure that you can *use* core counselling skills – not just know about them.

☑ Keep up to date with alternatives to traditional career paths.

☑ Remember that some clients' values will draw them to particular work *environments* as much as types of work role.

9 Self-management for Career Counsellors

In this chapter the monitoring and evaluation of practice, together with support and professional development for career counsellors, is addressed. The purpose of effective self-management in career counselling is similar to its purpose in other counselling contexts – to ensure that clients receive the best possible attention.

Everyone has their own individual flaws and blocks, and career counsellors should receive appropriate individual or group supervision to ensure that these do not adversely affect their work. Together with continued learning opportunities (perhaps through training and attending professional meetings), supervision is important for the career counsellor's development. Career counselling is a demanding occupation and counsellors need to look after themselves between, during and after sessions with clients. Good support is necessary from colleagues, to offload, to share areas of common interest, to pool knowledge and to reduce isolation. In addition, supervision plays a supportive role for the counsellor.

Constant self-monitoring and examination of the career counsellor's own work, which may usefully draw on feedback from clients, is also important.

Evaluation of career counselling

Monitoring and evaluating practice

Evaluating career counselling is a complex process because the results are not easily quantifiable. Killeen and Kidd (1991) reviewed a number of research studies examining the success of guidance (including counselling). The studies, mainly conducted on work with young people, showed outcomes such as increased certainty of a decision, improved decision-making skills and increased exploration of options.

What is the 'product' of successful career counselling? Some form of change. As we saw in the previous chapter, changes may be external (for example, a new job) or internal (new confidence, for instance). The following client did not get a new job but considered that his career counselling was very successful:

> Eric was a schoolteacher in his forties who came to career counselling to find out whether his dissatisfaction was due to his unsuitability for teaching. After several meetings and a number of tests, questionnaires and exercises, he came to the conclusion that teaching was basically the right area for him. Testing showed him to be rather passive, and part of his action plan at the final meeting was to go on an assertiveness course. He found this very useful, and a year later he reported that he was feeling more self-confident and settled. A career change was not the real solution; knowing his strengths and working on his weaknesses was.

Changes may not be easily attributable to the career counselling; a combination of factors, including the counselling, may lead to change. Although outcomes for the client may throw some light on the question 'Was the counselling successful?', we cannot evaluate the career counselling process solely on the basis of what the client has or has not been able to do because of the influence of other factors, such as the economic situation and unpredictable life events. When considering criteria for what constitutes success, we believe that what is important is not whether clients have 'reached a destination', but that they end by feeling in a position to 'continue the journey':

> Career counselling gave me the self-confidence to recognise that I had a lot to offer, which helped me to decide to do what I really wanted. This was not decided at the sessions, but was an ongoing process that stemmed from them.

Ultimately, the career counsellor can only really rely on his or her honest self-evaluation. This may be done in various ways:

- alone, by reflecting on your own practice, reviewing client notes and considering any evaluative feedback the client may have provided;
- using a 'session evaluation sheet' (see Box 9.1);
- with the help of peers, informally, in team meetings or group supervision;
- with the help of the manager of the service;
- with the help of an external supervisor; and
- through courses and professional meetings.

Box 9.1 Session evaluation sheet

- What did I do well?
- What could I have done differently?
- What did I learn from this session?
- What emotions were evoked in me?
- What is this client *really* expecting from me?
- How did I respond to the client's expectations of me?
- What were the blocks in me?
- And the client?
- Did I avoid giving advice?
- Did I work from the client's own starting point, taking into account individual circumstances and needs?
- Did I avoid stereotyping this client, that is, making assumptions on the basis of race, gender, social class, age, culture, sexuality, disability?
- If testing was used: did I offer feedback in a way which made the most positive use of the test information?
- If exercises were used: did I incorporate the most appropriate exercises in the most helpful way?

Evaluation by clients

Although evaluative feedback from clients is one source of information which the counsellor can consider in the process of self-evaluation, it is important not to rely on it as the only source. Feedback from clients is inevitably subjective. If life has improved, there may be a tendency to evaluate the career counselling positively. If life has not improved, one way of dealing with feelings of inadequacy is to project them on to the career counselling. Clients who have unresolved destructive and critical patterns of behaviour are likely to behave in that way with a feedback form too.

Evaluation should be a positive experience for the client. Inviting the client to evaluate the career counselling received helps to clarify and reinforce what has been gained, and keeps the momentum going (see pp. 106–7).

Some clients (especially those with a clearly delineated objective) may have achieved everything they wanted from career counselling by the end of the final meeting:

> Joseph had wanted to change career direction for a long time and had been through a careful process of considering his options before he came for career counselling. He wanted to assess his suitability for retraining as a physiotherapist. Understandably, he wanted to satisfy himself that he had the required attributes before he invested time and money in training. At the final meeting, Joseph was satisfied that he had achieved his objective, and went ahead with confidence to apply for courses in physiotherapy.

Such a totally successful outcome is rare. Many clients are at the very beginning of a longer process of continued self-understanding and exploration of options:

> Sylvia was 25 and had been unemployed for six months when she came for career counselling. Her education had been greatly disrupted by the death of her mother during her adolescence, and Sylvia's examination achievements were poor. She was also in the process of recovering from injuries sustained in a car accident and was feeling quite lonely and isolated. Career counselling showed her that she had far greater intellectual capabilities than she had expected. By the final meeting, she had decided that she would like to pursue her studies as a mature student, with a view to developing a career in the scientific or medical field. Her action plan covered a number of points, including researching different careers and courses, enquiring about her grant situation, building up her physical fitness, and developing new friendships.

When is the best time to evaluate?

Career counselling clients are in a process of transition, so changes may take place over an extended period of time in quite a subtle way. Immediately afterwards a client may not see the benefit, and may complain that they still don't know what to do, as the following case study demonstrates:

Tracey was asked to evaluate the career counselling shortly after her final meeting. At this meeting, the counsellor had reiterated the importance of making her own decision about what to do. The questionnaire asked about her expectations and the extent to which they had been met. She replied that she had wanted the counselling to point her in the 'right direction' and match her skills and qualities to suitable careers. She felt disappointed that this had not happened and felt she had been 'left up in the air'. She was clearly sceptical about the value of the counselling. A year later she was sent a follow-up questionnaire. She now felt that the career counselling had made 'a lot of difference' for her. She said that her objective of narrowing down her choice of career had been 'completely achieved'. She writes: 'The counselling takes time to sink in – without realizing it, I am in actual fact doing what was shown to be suited to me.' Based on all the job satisfaction criteria which the career counselling had helped her to identify, the job she was doing was giving her a high degree of satisfaction.

For people making complex changes in their lives, even a year is quite a short time-scale. We would recommend building into the career counselling contract an appropriate 'end point', when the effectiveness of the career counselling in achieving the agreed objectives can be evaluated. This would probably be *after* the client has had some time to implement and review any action plan.

Some useful questions which can be asked on an evaluation form are listed in Box 9.2.

Box 9.2 Client evaluation form

- What were your expectations of career counselling?
- To what extent have they been met?
- What in particular did you gain from career counselling?
- How could you have gained more from career counselling?
- Would you recommend the service to others?

Indicate the extent to which you agree or disagree with the following statements:
Career counselling helped me to:

- feel more confident;
- think more clearly about what I want from work;
- understand my strengths and weaknesses;
- decide on a plan for the future;
- narrow down my choice of occupation;
- link information about myself to possible jobs.

At a one-year follow-up, clients can be asked for details of any training undertaken, their current job, employer, main work functions and work responsibilities.

Personal and professional development

The process of monitoring and evaluating the career counselling will enable career counsellors to identify their personal and professional development needs. There are a number of ways of meeting these needs. Some are suggested in Box 9.3.

Box 9.3 Professional and personal development for career counsellors: some suggestions

- Further development of generic counselling skills, by attending, for example, short workshops or extended courses.
- Further development of specialist career counselling skills.
- Attending professional meetings, for example, in the UK:
  - British Association for Counselling and Psychotherapy (Association for Counselling at Work)
  - British Psychological Society – Counselling and Occupational Psychology sections
  - Institute of Careers Guidance
  - NICEC (National Institute for Careers Education and Counselling)
  - ACP International (Association of Careers Professionals); and
  - Counselling and Career Management Forum of the Chartered Institute of Personnel and Development.
- Attending careers conferences (for example, arranged by CRAC, the Careers Research Advisory Centre).
- Reading appropriate books and journals (see Appendices C and F).
- Obtaining counselling or therapy to work through personal issues (for career counsellors with issues relating to their own career satisfaction, success and achievement, obtaining career counselling or coaching may be appropriate).
- Occupational visits.
- Attending college open days.
- Supervision.

Supervision

Hess's (1980) commonly used definition of supervision describes it as an 'interpersonal interaction with the general goal that one person, the supervisor, meets with another, the supervisee, in an effort to make the latter more effective in helping people'. Supervision is a regular, structured opportunity for the career counsellor to examine his or her work. It has a threefold function of enabling the practitioner to learn and develop competence, to obtain support and encouragement, and to ensure good professional standards of practice. Proctor (1988) uses the terms 'formative', 'restorative' and 'normative' respectively for these functions.

Although some career counsellors will have supervision with their manager, we believe that this is no substitute for non-managerial supervision. Whether practised in groups or one to one, supervision is as essential a requirement for the career counsellor as it is for any other counsellor, as outlined in the British Association for Counselling and Psychotherapy's *Code of Ethics*. As in any counselling relationship, the confidentiality of client identity should be maintained.

Supervision can help career counsellors to obtain new perspectives, to assess the nature of the client's problem, to discuss the management of difficult cases, to assist in test interpretation, and to deal with feelings in relation to the client. In particular, it can help the counsellor to deal with the pressures of 'getting a result'. A client's anxiety for a solution is very contagious, and career counsellors often 'catch' it.

We believe that one-to-one supervision is especially appropriate at the stage when a career counsellor is 'learning the ropes'. If sessions with the client are tape-recorded (with the client's permission), the supervisor can listen to recordings and then discuss the work with the counsellor.

For the experienced career counsellor, we have found group approaches to supervision to be more beneficial, with counsellors taking turns to discuss their work. Such groups can be facilitated or peer-led. Although time management can be an issue, within a group there is a wider range of expertise to bring to bear on the career counsellor/client relationship being discussed. A co-counselling model where two counsellors 'exchange' supervision, taking turns to act as supervisor and supervisee, may also be appropriate for more experienced counsellors.

A group of three experienced career counsellors meet for one and a half hours every fortnight for supervision. At one of their meetings, the following issues were discussed.

Josephine described an initial meeting she had had with a highly disturbed and very angry client. She was able to offload her feelings of fear, and obtain reassurance from her colleagues about the course of action she had adopted, which was to recommend that the client see his doctor about being referred for psychotherapy.

Lorraine discussed her difficulties in counselling a client who had been sacked from his last three jobs. He had a history of being severely bullied at school. She realised through examining some feelings of revulsion towards him that some memories of her own difficulties at school were being triggered off. She also sought her colleagues' help in interpreting the meaning of the personality profile of one of her clients.

Doug brought two recent cases where both clients expected that he would have 'all the answers'. Just by talking through the pressures he felt, he realised that these clients were looking to him as a father figure, and he recognised the part in him which enjoyed being put on a pedestal.

Hawkins and Shohet (1989) have written comprehensively about models and processes of supervision in the helping professions generally, and the interested reader is referred to their book. A recent article (McMahon, 2003) noted the sporadic existence of supervision for career counsellors. Because of the many settings within which career counsellors work, and the varying degrees of emphasis given to the career counselling part of the work, we have observed that supervision more often takes the form of *supervisory activities*, such as ad hoc discussions with colleagues, attendance at professional development meetings and telephone and email support via professional networks.

For further discussion of the practice of counselling supervision, see Carroll (2001).

Self-management between and during sessions

Career counsellors need to be in as good mental and physical condition for the first and last clients of the day. One reason why people enter the caring professions is that they enjoy helping others. It is therefore hard to say 'no' when asked for help, but responding to caseload pressures by squeezing in more and more clients for even shorter appointments is a rapid route to, at best, inefficiency and, at worst, burnout. Often, counsellors do not realise the long-term damage they might be causing themselves and, in turn, that they will be providing a less professional service to clients. In a discussion of factors contributing to burnout, Nelson-Jones (1991) outlines the following causes:

- perfectionism;
- undue pessimism;
- unrealistically high goals;
- undue need for approval;
- inability to set limits on workload;
- poor time management;
- insufficient recreational outlets; and
- poor skills at looking after health and physical fitness.

Although Nelson-Jones was referring to people who run lifeskills training groups, these causes are equally pertinent to career counsellors. Some ways in which career counsellors can look after themselves between and during sessions are suggested in Box 9.4.

Box 9.4 Self-management for career counsellors between and during sessions

- Have at least a half-hour gap between clients, to allow for note taking, preparation and a non-counselling-related activity.
- Use the break between clients to attend to something quite different (for example, taking a walk, having a cup of tea or a chat with a colleague, doing a tension-reduction exercise).
- See no more than three or four clients a day, at one and a half hours each.
- Do not see individual clients all five days per week.
- Vary the kinds of work activity (for example, some 'group' work, balancing the daily workload with 'beginning, middle and end' meetings; doing something 'concrete' such as administration, research or arranging a meeting).

(Continued)

(Continued)

- Use a 'session evaluation sheet' (see Box 9.1) to highlight what has been achieved and learned in each session.
- Ask a colleague for some counselling time if left with any distressing feelings from a previous client and be prepared to share negative feelings, for example, of failure or powerlessness.
- Use the counselling skills of challenging and immediacy (see Egan, 2002) within sessions to avoid being trapped into destructive transference and countertransference problems.
- Have an icon within sight which evokes feelings of peace or serenity, for example, a photograph, picture, flower or favourite saying.

One tension-reduction exercise is to completely flop in your chair, allowing all your muscles to collapse as you reach for the floor. Then, after about one minute, slowly revert to your sitting position.

Another way in which career counsellors in some (but not all) settings can look after themselves is by not feeling obliged to take on all clients who are requesting career counselling. A career counsellor may not feel able or willing to take on a particular client, perhaps because the client and counsellor hold such opposing values that the counsellor finds it impossible to listen to and empathise with the client. It is worth addressing this dilemma before becoming committed to a series of unproductive and draining meetings. It might be feasible to build into a contract some kind of 'opt out' clause, so that either client or counsellor can withdraw after the first meeting if either feels unable to work with the other.

Above all, it is important to avoid becoming trapped into colluding with a client's desire for you to provide an answer. As we have seen, this is an especially prevalent expectation in career counselling. Neither is it the career counsellor's responsibility to ensure that the client gets a job. A client may have a legitimate need to find a job quickly to pay for essential living requirements, but this should not detract from the goals of career counselling established at the beginning of the contract. These will probably focus on resolving some of the pressures brought about by the need to earn a living in relation to the personal desire for a satisfying occupation. Such a resolution may not be achieved within the counselling meetings, but it may evolve when a client has had a chance to test out some of the ideas developed in the career counselling.

Summary

We have devoted this entire chapter to the topic of self-management for career counsellors, as it is an area so easy to overlook on account of day-to-day pressures. Self-care needs to be a priority for several reasons:

- career counselling is a demanding occupation;
- if the career counsellor is in good 'shape', clients will benefit; and
- the chances of career counsellor 'burnout' are lessened.

Such self-management goes on between, during and after sessions. Evaluating the quality of outcomes from the career counselling is a way of both client and career counsellor gaining a sense of completion. Supervision or 'supervisory activities' can enable career counsellors to 'see' their way more clearly through any blocks with clients, as well as gain support in an otherwise quite isolated occupation.

Checklist: Self-management for career counsellors

☑ Remind yourself that self-management needs to be a priority to do effective career counselling work.

☑ If you enable clients to 'continue their journey' (rather than 'arrive at their destination'), this can be an important outcome.

☑ Be prepared to monitor the effectiveness of your work continually – make use of a 'session evaluation sheet'.

☑ Remember that a combination of factors, including the career counselling, may lead to change.

☑ Make evaluation a positive experience for the client; use it to enable clients to clarify and reinforce what has been gained, and keep the momentum going.

☑ Remind yourself, and your clients, that changes following the career counselling can take place over an extended period.

☑ Build into the career counselling contract an appropriate 'end point', when its effectiveness in achieving the agreed objectives can be evaluated.

☑ Regularly attend meetings of professional groups, and use coaching or counselling to acknowledge and manage your personal issues that may be restricting your effectiveness as a career counsellor.

☑ Use one-to-one or group 'non-managerial supervision' to address, confidentially, any anxieties you have about particular clients.

☑ Recognise your 'self-destructive patterns' of behaviour, such as 'perfectionism' or 'difficulty in saying "no"'.

☑ Don't collude with a client's desire to find 'the answer'.

Appendix A: Guidelines for Tests

These 'guidelines' can be given to clients at the end of the first meeting, where aptitude or ability tests are to be given.

Testing is a part of the process of career counselling which provides helpful information about you by making an objective assessment of your aptitudes. These tests are objective; they have been given to thousands of people. This ensures that the information they provide is useful and valid.

Tests play an important part, but need to be seen in the whole context of career counselling. They are just one source of information about you, and their results will not be accepted blindly at face value. The other questionnaires you complete, covering interests and personality, can yield information at least of equal importance, as can any other exercises given to you by your career counsellor. Although aptitude tests are objective, they can be affected by your feelings, and anxiety, on the day.

Your career counsellor will help you to understand how such factors may have affected you, when you discuss the results together.

Test administration

The tests may seem rather like an exam because they are accurately timed and carried out under fixed conditions and because there may be another person or other people doing the tests at the same time as you. However, they are *not* competitive and are purely a way of finding out about you.

The aptitude test session lasts for about three hours and is broken down into a number of shorter tests, with a break in the middle. After a 45-minute break for lunch, you will have a number of short, untimed questionnaires to fill out as well. These will take you from two to three hours.

Appendix B: Action Plan

Action plan

Be clear about your goal (where you want to be).

1   My goal is:

Consider the gap between where you are now and where you want to be, and the steps you will need to take to bridge the gap. List the most useful 'action steps' (what you need to do to achieve your goal) without worrying about their sequence. Be very specific about what each step involves.

2   My action steps are:

3   Number the action steps in a logical sequence.

4   Write down your plan:

   Tomorrow I will …

   Over the next week I will …

   Over the next month I will …

   Over the next three months I will …

   Over the next six months I will …

5   Decide when you will review progress:

   My review date will be …

Appendix C: Sources of Occupational Information

Clients can access up-to-date information about careers, employers and job availability via the Internet, newspapers, professional journals, professional and trade associations, recruitment brochures, books, videos, CDs, DVDs and other publications. It can be confusing to know where to start. Once clients have a reasonably clear idea of their career goals, it is advisable to furnish them with a list of appropriate information resources. Since many libraries, professional bodies and employers carry excellent information online, the actual *location* of the institution may be of minimal importance. If clients wish to access local information, but are in a location remote from that source, we suggest first using any online resources and then following up with specific requests by email. We start by listing a few key UK-based libraries.

Libraries

Two specialist libraries that stock relevant material for job hunters researching employers (for example, annual reports, business and trade journals, contact directories) are:

The City Business Library, 1 Brewers' Hall Garden, London EC2V 5BX. Tel: 020 7332 1812. Has a fee-paying business research service for anyone not able to conduct their own research.

British Library (Business Collections), St Pancras, 96 Euston Road, London NW1 2DB. Tel: 020 7412 7677 (for Reader Admissions). Access is open to all. Take proof of identity for a reader's card. Has access to COBRA – the Complete Business Reference Adviser database for people setting up or running a small business. Reading rooms also in Boston Spa, Yorkshire and Colindale, North London.

Both these libraries have extensive collections (for example, business trend information, trade journals, market research, directories) and staff who can help customers find what they need. Some of their catalogues are available online.

Another good reference library for business is:

Business Insight, Central Library, Chamberlain Square, Birmingham B3 3HQ. Tel: 0121 303 4531. For non-Birmingham-based inquirers, all information is carried on their website: www.bestforbusiness.com.

Information and advice services available for the public

Even in the UK, the provision of these services varies. In England, there is a cut-off age of 19 for provision of 'information, advice and guidance'. Some areas provide a separate service for adults. In Scotland, services are more integrated. For more detailed information about services available in your country or region, use the following weblinks:

Wales: www.careerswales.com
Scotland: www.careers-scotland.org.uk
Northern Ireland: www.egsa.org.uk
England: www.nextstep.org.uk
UK learning advice: www.learndirect.co.uk

Careers information and job search websites

Clients should use websites not just for the information contained in them, but for the links they open up to other sites and sources of information. Whilst the following recommended sites are UK-based, some will link the user to a much wider base of information about work opportunities worldwide.

Careers information

www.support4learning.org.uk/careers/advisers.htm
Excellent resource site for anyone working in careers support.

www.prospects.ac.uk
Relevant to anyone seeking information on careers, although target audience is graduates. Easy-to-access alphabetical listings of occupations.

www.connexions.gov.uk/jobs4u/catalogue.cfm
Information on wide range of jobs, from bricklayer to brain surgeon. Help with job ideas.

www.learndirect-futures.co.uk
Contains tools to match skills and experience to jobs and career choice.

www.graduatecareers.hobsons.co.uk
Graduate careers information about employers and jobs.

www.trotman.co.uk
Click the 'careers portal' link for career information and more.

www.worktrain.gov.uk
UK government site giving information on childcare and voluntary opportunities. Links to wide range of careers sites (for example, BBC).

www.waytolearn.co.uk
UK government site with information on qualifications needed for different careers, funding information and more.

www.ukcoursefinder.com
Comprehensive higher education directory.

www.doctorjob.co.uk
Wide-ranging careers information.

www.channel4.com/brilliantcareers
Lively website with some careers information.

Vacancy and job market statistics

www.jobs.guardian.co.uk
A mixture of vacancy information and careers advice. Many national newspapers offer similar sites.

www.nomisweb.co.uk
Regional employment and labour market information in the UK. Search by postcode.

www.statistics.gov.uk
Labour market data detailed by industry, full- and part-time jobs. Also carries information on employment by age.

www.insidecareers.co.uk
Information and job vacancies in IT and related areas.

www.monster.co.uk
International and UK job vacancies.

www.careersforleaders.com
Vacancies in the public and not-for-profit sectors.

www.fishforjobs.co.uk
Broad-based vacancies.

www.gisajob.com
Broad database of vacancies in UK and worldwide.

Note that many employers now recruit via their websites.

Professional bodies

A large number of professional bodies and trade associations produce careers information, much of which is provided at little or no cost to the enquirer. The CIOLA (Connexions and Careers Information Officers Link Association) directory (Trotman, 2005), *The Essential Guide to Careers and Connexions Information Resources*, provides a comprehensive listing of these organisations – look under 'Information sources'.

Reference books

For career counsellors, some of the most useful publications for reference include:

Occupations (DfES, annual)
Careers 2006 (Trotman, 2005)
The Careers and Personal Advisers Handbook (A. Dixon ed., Trotman, 2003)
Jobfile: The Essential Careers Handbook (P. Herington and J. Frankcom eds, Careers Management, 2005)
British Qualifications (H. Davison ed., Kogan Page, 2005)
Second Chances (Careers and Occupational Information Centre, annual)
Mature Students Directory (M. Flynn ed., Trotman, 2004)
The Mid-career Action Guide: A Practical Guide to Mid-career Change (D. and F. Kemp, Kogan Page, 1991)
The Penguin Careers Guide (J. Widmer, Penguin, 2004)
The A–Z of Careers and Jobs (J. Poynter, Kogan Page, 2004)

Guides to specific careers

A number of publishers produce guides to specific careers, each of which describes the nature of the work, together with details of entry and training.

Examples of websites giving information on specific careers:

www.skillset.org
Information and advice on media careers. Links to other relevant sites.

www.lantra.co.uk
Information on environmental careers.

Less conventional guides

The Career Guide for Creative and Unconventional People (C. Eikleberry, Ten Speed Press, 1999)

Odd Jobs: Unusual Ways to Earn a Living (S. Kent, Kogan Page, 2002)

Cool Careers for Dummies (M. Nemko, P. Edwards and S. Edwards, IDG, 1998)

Do What You Are (P.D. Tieger and B. Barron-Tieger, Little, Brown, 2001)

The Work We Were Born to Do (N. Williams, Element, 1999)

Careers Un-ltd (J. Robinson and C. McConnell, Pearson Education, 2003)

The Everything Alternative Careers Book: Leave the Office Behind and Embark on a New Adventure (J. Mannion, Adams, 2004)

Women

Back to Work: A Guide for Women Returners (D. Wolfin and S. Foreman, Robson, 2004)

Careers and Motherhood, Challenges and Choices: How to Successfully Manage your Career through Pregnancy, Birth and Motherhood (K. Mitchell, McGraw Hill Education, 2004)

Career change

The Career Change Handbook (G. Green, How to Books, 2003)

Lawyers' Career Change Handbook (H. Greenberg, Quill, 2002)

Changing Your Career: Practical Advice to Help you Move on (S. Longson, Kogan Page, 2003)

What Can I Do with No Degree? (M. McAlpine, Trotman, 2004)

Fearless Career Change (M. Stein, McGraw Hill, 2005)

Job search

Great Answers to Tough Interview Questions (M.J. Yate, Kogan Page, 1992)

The London Jobhunter's Guide 2003/4 (T. Gough and F. Fitzsimons, Pearson Education, 2003)

Self-employment

Hindsight: From Starting up to Successful Entrepreneur, by Those Who've Been There (R. Branson and R. Thackray, Virgin Business Guides, 2002)

Anyone Can Do It (S. and B. Hashemi, Capstone, 2002)

www.shell-livewire.org (helps 16 to 30-year-olds start up in business)

The Small Business Handbook: An Entrepreneur's Definitive Guide to Starting a Business and Growing a Business (P. and S. Webb, Prentice Hall, 2001)

Self-help workbooks

These publications contain exercises that can be used by individuals who want to further their career development. To gain maximum benefit from them, some discussion of the exercises is necessary, so workbooks are best used as an adjunct to career counselling.

What Colour Is Your Parachute? (R.N. Bolles, Ten Speed Press, 1998)

The Lotus and the Pool: How to Create Your Own Career (H.L. Dail, Shambhala Publications, 1989)

Build Your Own Rainbow: A Workbook for Career and Life Management (B. Hopson and M. Scaily, Management Books, 1999)

Who Do You Think You Are? Understanding Your Motives and Maximising Your Abilities (N. Isbister and M. Robinson, Zondervan, 1999)

How to Get a Job You'll Love (J. Lees, McGraw Hill Professional, 2005)

The CCS Self-assessment Manual (R. Nathan and J. Floyed, Career Counselling Services, 2002 – available under licence only)

Springboard: Women's Development Workbook (L. Willis and J. Daisley, Hawthorn Press, 2000)

Recruitment agencies

For details of recruitment agencies, consult:

www.rec.uk.com. Website of the Recruitment and Employment Federation. Gives details of member recruitment consultants.

The Personnel Manager's Yearbook (AP Information Services, annual). Contains a modest listing.

www.executive-grapevine.co.uk. Executive Grapevine publishes the *UK and International Directories of Executive Recruitment Consultants*.

Appendix D: The Use of Software to Support Career Counselling

Modern careers software enables career counsellors and their clients to access a huge range of information. The advantage of specific careers software over the Internet is that the information it contains may be more precisely tailored to the needs of the user. Some clients may become bewildered by the array of information on the Internet. A few providers are mentioned below. For a more complete list, refer to the annual publication *CIOLA – The Essential Guide to Careers and Connexions Information Resources* (see p. 154).

Career builder

Self-assessment exercises linked to occupational suggestions:
www.stuartmitchellassociates.co.uk

Careers information database

Suitable for all ages: www.careersoft.co.uk

Careers match

Matches interests and qualifications to careers: http://www.cascaid.co.uk/CMW3C/Start.jsp

Europe in the round

Information on working in the European Union: www.gesvt.com

Work trends

Information on labour market trends, including sources of job vacancies:
www.careersoft.co.uk

Appendix E: Training Courses

Some UK-based courses in career counselling are listed here. Qualifications are specific to career counselling and career guidance work.

- Postgraduate Diploma in Careers Guidance (DCG): Can lead on to MA in Careers Guidance.
- MSc Career Management and Counselling (available only at Birkbeck College, London University): Network learning and workshops over two years; can lead to work in private or public sectors, see www.bbk.ac.uk
- Qualification in Careers Guidance (QCG)
- S/NVQ Level 4 in Advice and Guidance: Contact the Institute of Career Guidance (see below) for information.
- The CCS Core Skills Career Counselling Training Course: Practical five-day programme over two modules, leading to licence to use CCS Self-assessment Manual materials. Open to people currently using counselling skills in their work, see www. career-counselling-services.co.uk.

Professional bodies

Institute of Career Guidance (ICG)
Third Floor
Copthall House
1 New Road
Stourbridge
West Midlands DY8 1PH
Tel: 01384 376464
www.icg-uk.org

National Association for Educational Guidance for Adults (NAEGA)
PO Box 459
Belfast BT2 8YA
Tel: 028 9027 1509
www.naega.org.uk

National Institute for Careers Education and Counselling (NICEC)
Sheraton House
Castle Park
Cambridge CB3 0AX
Tel: 01223 460277
www.crac.org.uk/nicec/nicec.htm

Appendix F: Relevant Journals

British Journal of Guidance and Counselling. Cambridge: CRAC

Career Development International. Bradford: Emerald Group

Career Development Quarterly. Alexandria, VA: AACD

Counselling and Psychotherapy Journal. Rugby: BACP

The Counselling Psychologist. London: Sage

HR Magazine. Alexandria, VA: Society for Human Resource Management

International Journal of Human Resource Management. London: Routledge

International Journal of Training and Development. Oxford: Blackwell

Journal of Occupational and Organisational Psychology. Leicester: BPS

Journal of Organisational Behaviour. Chichester: Wiley

Journal of Vocational Behavior. San Diego, CA: Academic Press

People Management (Journal of the CIPD). London: Institute of Personnel Management

Personnel Review. Bradford: Emerald Group

Appendix G: Useful Organisations

Association of Graduate Careers Advisory Staff (AGCAS)
Millennium House
30 Junction Road
Sheffield
S11 8XB
Tel: +44 (0)114 251 5750
www.agcas.org.uk
(See website for various email contacts.)

Brief Therapy Practice
7–8 Newbury Street
London EC1A 7HU
Tel: +44 (0)20 7600 3366
www.brieftherapy.org.uk
solutions@brieftherapy.org.uk
(Offers training in solution-focused counselling.)

British Association for Counselling and Psychotherapy (BACP)
BACP House
35–7 Albert Street
Rugby
Warwickshire CV2I 2SG
Tel: +44 (0)1788 550899
www.bacp.co.uk
bacp@bacp.co.uk

British Psychological Society (BPS)
Occupational Psychology Section
St Andrews House
48 Princess Road East
Leicester LE1 7DR
Tel: +44 (0)116 254 9568
www.bps.org.uk
enquiry@bps.org.uk

Career Counselling Services
46 Ferry Road
London SW13 9PW

Tel: +44 (0)20 8741 0335
www.career-counselling-services.co.uk
careercs@dial.pipex.com

Careers Research and Advisory Centre (CRAC)
Sheraton House
Castle Park
Cambridge CB3 0AX
Tel: +44 (0)1223 460 277
www.crac.org.uk
web.enquiries@crac.org.uk

CCDU Training & Consultancy
University of Leeds
Woodhouse Lane
Leeds LS2 9JT
Tel: +44 (0)113 394 3900
www.ccdu.co.uk
ccdu@ccdu.york.com

Chartered Institute of Personnel and Development (CIPD)
Career Management and Counselling Forum
151 The Broadway
London SW19 1JQ
Tel: +44 (0)20 8612 6200
www.cipd.co.uk
cipd@cipd.co.uk

The Guidance Council
Renaissance House
20 Princess Road West
Leicester LEI 6TP
Tel: (from UK only) 0870 774 3744
www.guidancecouncil.com
feedback@guidancecouncil.com

Institute of Careers Guidance (ICG)
Third Floor
Copthall House
I New Road
Stourbridge
West Midlands DY8 1PH
Tel: +44 (0)1384 376464
www.icg-uk.org
abody@icg-uk.org

Learning and Skills Council
National Office

Cheylesmore House
Quinton Road
Coventry CV21 2WT
Tel: +44 (0)845 019 4170
www.lsc.gov.uk
info@lsc.gov.uk

Pilat (UK) Limited
29 Hendon Lane
London N3 1PZ
Tel: +44 (0)20 8343 3433
www.pilat.com
info@pilat.com
(For 360-degree feedback.)

Qualifications and Curriculum Authority (QCA)
83 Piccadilly
London WIJ 8QA
Tel: +44 (0)20 7509 5555
www.qca.org.uk
info@qca.org.uk

Appendix H: Career Counselling Exercises

The exercises described in this book are drawn from *The CCS (Career Counselling Services) Self-assessment Manual*. Versions suitable for photocopying and handing to your client for completion are available to download from www.sagepub.co.uk/resources/careercounselling.pdf.

The following are the settings where the exercises may be useful:

- one-to-one counselling or coaching;
- career planning workshops;
- job search support;
- personal development workshops;
- development centres;
- stress management workshops;
- managing personal/career change programmes;
- interpersonal skills development.

Inappropriate use of the exercises

Many people, clients and career counsellors may be tempted to use 'an exercise' that *seems* relevant. The framework it provides, as well as its content, may seem sufficient to enable clients to do the 'work' themselves, without talking it through. Such an approach is fraught with dangers. These include:

- what is written down by the client may merely repeat prior thoughts;
- the lack of professional career counselling to talk through the responses may lead the client round in circles; and
- one exercise may be seen initially as a panacea.

Clients may not be sufficiently prepared for undertaking the exercise as part of a career counselling process. Hence, while interesting, the result may be one of disappointment and a consequent loss of faith in such exercises for the future (we have experienced some clients who have repeatedly attempted exercise after exercise, with increasingly sophisticated, but futile, attempts to analyse and make sense of the 'data'). In certain cases, an exercise could raise uncomfortable feelings. Without professional support to talk these through, the result could compound the client's sense of 'stuckness'.

Because of these potential dangers, these exercises should not be distributed as part of a 'self-help' workbook or placed on an Intranet site without appropriate positioning as part of a supported career counselling process.

Guidelines for using the exercises

- Use *only* in conjunction with individual or workshop-based career counselling.
- Ensure that you have read through the text of the book where the exercise is described.
- You should be confident enough to deal with the emotions that some exercises may engender. This confidence is most likely to be gained from a combination of experience and training (see Appendix E). A good way to begin is to complete the exercise and talk it through with a colleague trained in career counselling.
- Position each exercise according to its particular objective, as well as its role in relation to any other exercises.
- Try suggesting that 'we will be looking for patterns arising from several exercises'.
- Choose exercises you believe the client will be successful in completing.
- Ensure that the client 'owns' the exercise (that is, does not treat it as 'homework' to be handed in for assessment).
- Remember that, if clients do not complete an exercise, they may have thought about what it asks for but not been able to commit to paper. Give them time to talk it through.

The exercises are organised in five stages:

- Exploring
  (Who am I?)
- Clarifying
  (What do I want?)
- Identifying options
- What stops me/can help me move forward?
- Action planning

Exploring

Enjoyable events (see p. 54)

Objective: To identify what you have found enjoyable in all parts of your life.

Instructions: Using the table below, list the three to four most enjoyable events/ experiences in (any part of) your life. These should be specific events/experiences, not a general statement of what you have enjoyed. Then in the other two columns write down:

a) What you enjoyed.
b) What you gained or learned, if anything, from each event or experience.

Review the exercise with your career counsellor, a colleague or a friend, high-lighting patterns of what you enjoyed and what you gained and learned.

Complete the comments column of the table. Were there any surprises? Were most of your events at work or outside of work? How consistent were these patterns with your current or last position? What are the implications of these patterns?

Enjoyable events		
Events	**What I found enjoyable**	**What I gained or learned**
1		
2		
3		
4		
Comments/Surprises/Implications/Patterns:		

An A4 version of this form is available to print out from www.sagepub.co.uk/resources/career counselling.pdf

Satisfying achievements (see pp. 55–6)
Objective: To establish patterns of:

- achievements you have found satisfying;
- what you found satisfying about those achievements; and
- skills you used in attaining those achievements.

Instructions: Using the table below, list the three to four most satisfying achievements from (any part of) your life. These should be specific achievements, and not general statements of what you have found satisfying. Then in the other two columns write down:

a) What you found satisfying.
b) What skills and other qualities you used in each achievement.

   Review the exercise with your career counsellor, a colleague or friend, highlighting any patterns of achievements and skills which you may have missed.
   Complete the comments column of the table. Were there any surprises? What are the implications of these patterns for you?

Satisfying achievements		
Achievements	**What I found satisfying**	**The skills and qualities I used**
1		
2		
3		
4		
Comments/Surprises/Implications/Patterns:		

An A4 version of this form is available to print out from www.sagepub.co.uk/resources/career counselling.pdf

Clarifying
Job satisfiers (see pp. 61–3)
Objective: To evaluate the elements of job satisfaction most important to you.

Instructions:

1   List below in any order those elements of work you must have in your next job. Be specific. You could think of 'tasks' (what you will do), 'people' (who with), 'environment' (in what type of organisation) and 'rewards' (pay, working conditions and so on).

Example:
Minimal management responsibility
Using my creativity
Improving people's lot in some way
Little routine
Working with intelligent, non-conformist people
A small, forward-looking organisation
No less than £25k at current rates

Try and keep your list to 12 elements. Write them below:

My elements of job satisfaction:	
1	7
2	8
3	9
4	10
5	11
6	12

2   Look again at the 'job satisfiers' you have listed in the previous table. Answer the question: 'Which is more important to me – number 1 or 2?' If you answer number 1, for example, circle the figure '1' in the first column. Then proceed for every pair of job satisfiers – 1-3, 1-4, 1-5 and so on, until 11-12. Work quickly. Some 'satisfiers' may overlap, nevertheless make a choice.

1–2	2–3	3–4	4–5	5–6	6–7	7–8	8–9	9–10	10–11	11–12
1–3	2–4	3–5	4–6	5–7	6–8	7–9	8–10	9–11	10–12	
1–4	2–5	3–6	4–7	5–8	6–9	7–10	8–11	9–12		
1–5	2–6	3–7	4–8	5–9	6–10	7–11	8–12			
1–6	2–7	3–8	4–9	5–10	6–11	7–12				
1–7	2–8	3–9	4–10	5–11	6–12					
1–8	2–9	3–10	4–11	5–12						
1–9	2–10	3–11	4–12							
1–10	2–11	3–12								
1–11	2–12									
1–12										

Count up the number of circles for each job satisfier. This is your 'weighted' score. Write down the scores next to each job satisfier.

4   Discuss this exercise with your career counsellor, colleague or friend.
5   List your three top job satisfiers:

1

2

3

Identifying options

Generating job ideas
Objective: To expand your ideas about work possibilities.

Introduction: To make a decision about your best course of action, you need self-knowledge, some sense of purpose (not your exact direction) and knowledge of the options available. You may want a similar job to your last one. However, there are many other possibilities open to you. You should be aware of these before dismissing anything.

Some alternative ideas to a conventional 'full-time job' are listed below:

- part-time work (possibly combining two options);
- consultancy/short-term contracts/interim management (increasingly in demand);
- freelance work (for example, specialist writing);
- self-employment (could work from home or a business centre);
- temporary work (usually through employment agency);
- franchising (for example, Prontaprint);
- co-operatives (a common-ownership working structure);
- seasonal work (for example, grape picking);
- casual work (for example, reception, pub work, data input);
- voluntary work (could be useful to gain experience);
- working abroad (could help with language skills);
- combining travel and work (for example, ship's hairdresser);
- stepping-stone work (gives you necessary experience for more fulfilling work).

Whilst some of the above may be useful time-fillers, others could be an alternative way of managing your career, perhaps even preferable to you.

Instructions:
1 Write down any work ideas you have, no matter how fanciful. Include training courses if you like. If you get stuck, ask a friend or colleague to prompt you. Ask for ideas from as many people as you can. Look in the index of a careers book or try one or two websites. We recommend the following:

   The Penguin Careers Guide (J. Widmer, Penguin, 2004)
   Grad File (Careers Management, 2001)
   Occupations (DfES, annual).

   These titles should be available in your local Reference or Careers Library.

   www.careers.lon.ac.uk, University of London careers information site (excellent links)
   www.prospects.ac.uk, graduate level careers information
   www.doctorjob.co.uk, wide-ranging careers information

Write your ideas below:

1	11
2	12
3	13
4	14
5	15
6	16
7	17
8	18
9	19
10	20

2   Now list the options under the following three headings:

- 'Similar' – ideas similar to the job(s) you have already done.
- 'Complementary' – ideas related to the work you have done.
- 'Breakthrough' – job ideas which are completely different.

Similar	Complementary	Breakthrough

3   Evaluate each of the most attractive options in terms of benefits and risks.

Idea	Benefits	Risks
Example: Do writing course with view to part-time journalism	1 Always wanted to do it. 2 Develop new skill. 3 I'd enjoy it.	1 Might distract me from job hunting. 2 Hard to get contacts.
1		
2		
3		
4		
5		

4   Discuss this exercise with a colleague or friend.
5   List below the options most attractive, in spite of the risks:

1

2

3

What stops me/can help me move forward?

Blocks and bridges (see pp. 64–6)

Objective: To identify those resources in your life which may help or hinder you in achieving your goals.

Instructions: Using the form below, write down your 'Bridges' – the internal and external resources you currently have which would help you achieve your goals. Typical bridges include skills, qualifications, training, experience, contacts, knowledge, motivation, self-belief, money, support from people and your own personal qualities. Similarly, list your 'blocks', which could include a lack of certain resources.

  Talk though the blocks and bridges with your career counsellor, colleague or a friend. How real are they? How could they be overcome? Which ones could not be? Could some of your bridges help you overcome a block? If some cannot be overcome, what could you do? (Often an increased awareness of blocks can help to minimise their impact).

Blocks and bridges	
My goal:	
Blocks	Bridges

An A4 version of this form is available to print out from www.sagepub.co.uk/resources/career counselling.pdf

Action planning
Setting objectives (see p. 151)
Objective: To set some realistic and achievable career and personal development objectives.

Introduction: New Year's resolutions often last less than a week or two. Why? Because they are usually made in haste and with insufficient commitment. They may well be unrealistic and too general, for example, 'I want to stop drinking'. Similarly, a career objective such as 'I plan to become a manager' is no more than a statement of intent. This exercise will assist you to narrow down your intentions to more precise objectives.

Instructions: In the table on p. 175, write in column 1 a general statement of intent. Then, following discussion with your career counsellor, complete columns 2 and 3 (see the example).

Complete columns 4, 5 and 6, headed 'My commitment', 'How realistic?' and 'By when?'. Rate your commitment to the statements you write in column 3 on a 1 to 10 scale (1 = not at all committed, 10 = completely committed).

Rate the degree to which you believe the objective is a realistic one (1 = highly unrealistic, 10 = utterly realistic). Write in a date by which you intend to achieve each objective in column 3.

Rewrite any objectives (or discard them) if they are either unrealistic or if your commitment is questionable (less than 8). Or think of ways to increase the chances of achieving the objective by breaking it down further into realistic 'bite-sized' chunks which may be more attractive to you.

Highlight (or underline) the objectives you plan to pursue. Decide on a date at which you will review your progress. Write this in brackets in column 6. At this point, you may want to modify some of your objectives.

Tick or cross through the objective when you have achieved it to your satisfaction.

Column 1 Statement of intent	Column 2 How?	Column 3 How?	Column 4 My commitment 1–10	Column 5 How realistic? 1–10	Column 6 By when?
Example					
I want to become a manager.	By changing jobs.	Talk to HR manager.	10	10	30 June
	By getting trained.	Find out about DMS courses.	9	10	31 May
		Deputising for boss.	7	6	31 December
1					
2					
3					
4					
5					

An A4 version of this form is available to print out from www.sagepub.co.uk/resources/career counselling.pdf

References

Abbey, L. and Graham, B. (1996) *A Counselling Approach to Career Guidance*. London: Routledge.

Adams, J., Hayes, J. and Hopson, B. (1976) *Understanding and Managing Personal Change*. London: Martin Robertson.

Allen, C.A. (1975) 'Life planning: its purpose and position in the human potential movement'. MA thesis, University of Leeds.

Allen, D. (2002) *Getting Things Done: The Art of Stress-free Productivity*. London: Piatkus.

Anastasi, A. (1988) *Psychological Testing*. New York: Macmillan.

Arnold, J. (1997) *Managing Careers into the 21st Century*. London: Paul Chapman.

Arthur, M.B., Hall, D.T. and Lawrence, B.S. (eds) (1989) *Handbook of Career Theory*. Cambridge: Cambridge University Press.

Bandura, A. (1977) 'Self-efficacy: toward a unifying theory of behavioral change', *Psychological Bulletin*, 84: 191–215.

Berne, E. (1968) *Games People Play*. Harmondsworth: Penguin.

Bridges, W. (1995) *Managing Transitions*. London: Nicholas Brealey.

British Association for Counselling and Psychotherapy (2004) *Code of Ethics and Practice for Counsellors*. Rugby: BACP.

British Association for Counselling and Psychotherapy (annual) *Counselling and Psychotherapy Resources Directory*. Rugby: BAC. http://www.bacp.co.uk/seeking_therapist/index.html

Carroll, M. (2001) *Counselling Supervision*. London: Sage.

CIOLA Directory (2005) *The Adviser's Guide to Careers Information Resources*. Richmond: Trotman.

Clarkson, P. (2003) *How to Overcome Your Secret Fear of Failure*. London: Vega.

Clarkson, P. (2004) *Gestalt Counselling in Action*. London: Sage.

Clay, J. (1989) *Men at Midlife: The Facts, the Fantasies, the Future*. London: Sidgwick and Jackson.

Cochran, L. (1997) *Career Counselling: A Narrative Approach*. London: Sage.

Collin, A. (1979) 'Mid-life crisis and its implications in counselling', *British Journal of Guidance and Counselling*, 7(2): 144–52.

Corcoran, M., Duncan, G. and Hill, M. (1984) 'The economic fortunes of women and children: lessons from the panel study on income dynamics', *Signs: Journal of Women in Culture and Society*, 10: 232–48.

Dail, H.L. (1989) *The Lotus and the Pool: How to Create Your Own Career*. Boston, MA: Sharnbhala.

Dryden, W. (1979) 'Rational-emotive therapy and its contribution to careers counselling', *British Journal of Guidance and Counselling*, 7(2): 181–7.

Egan, G. (2002) *The Skilled Helper: A Problem-Management and Opportunity-Development Approach to Helping*. Pacific Grove, CA: Brooks/Cole.

Ellis, A. (1962) *Reason and Emotion in Psychotherapy*. New York: Lyle Stuart.

Erikson, E. (1971) *Identity: Youth and Crisis*. London: Faber and Faber.

Flloyed, J. and Nathan, R. (2002) *The CCS Job Hunting Manual*. London: Career Counselling Services.

Ford, G. (2002) 'The connexions strategy and all-age guidance'. Occasional paper, Centre for Guidance Studies, University of Derby.

Francis, D. (1985) *Managing Your Own Career*. London: Collins.

Greene, J. and Grant, A.M. (2003) *Solution-focussed Coaching*. Harlow: Pearson Education.

Hashemi, S. and Hashemi, B. (2002) *Anyone Can Do It*. Oxford: Capstone.

Hawkins, P. and Shohet, R. (1989) *Supervision in the Helping Professions*. Milton Keynes: Open University Press.

Hawthorn, R. (1991) *Who Offers Guidance*. Sheffield: Employment Department.

Heron, J. (1990) *Helping the Client: A Creative Practical Guide*. London: Sage.

Herriot, P. (1992) *The Career Management Challenge: Balancing Individual and Organisational Needs*. London: Sage.

Hess, A.K. (ed.) (1980) *Psychotherapy Supervision: Theory, Research and Practice*. New York: Wiley.

Hirsch, W. (2002) 'Careers in organisations – time to get positive', in *The Future of Careers*. London: CIPD.

Hirsch, W. (2003) *Straight Talking: Effective Career Discussions at Work*. London: NICEC.

Hirsch, W. and Jackson, C. (2004) *Managing Careers in Large Organisations*. London: NICEC.

Hirsch W., Jackson, C. and Kidd, J.M. (2001) *Straight Talking: Effective Career Discussions at Work*. London: NICEC/CRAC.

Holland, J.L. (1983) *Making Vocational Choices: A Theory of Careers*. Englewood Cliffs, NJ: Prentice-Hall.

Hopson, B. and Scally, M. (1991) *Build Your Own Rainbow: A Workbook for Career and Life Management*. Leeds: Lifeskills Associates.

Jacinto, C., Woo, R. and Elmer, E. (2000) *Psychodynamic Approaches to Career Counselling*. http://www.eddyelmer.com/tools/pagestart.html?http://www.eddyelmer.com/tools/career.htm

Jackson, C. (1990) *Careers Counselling in Organisations: The Way Forward*. IMS Report 198. Brighton: Institute of Employment Studies.

Killeen, J.F. and Kidd, J.M. (1991) *Learning Outcomes of Guidance: A Review of Recent Research*. Sheffield: Employment Department.

King, Z. (2004) *Career Management – A Guide*. London: CIPD.

Krumboltz, J.D. (1976) 'A social learning theory of career selection', *The Counselling Psychologist*, 6(1): 71–81.

Levinson, D.J., Darrow, C., Klein, E., Levinson, M. and McKee, B. (1978) *The Seasons of a Man's Life*. New York: Knopf.

London, M. and Stumpf, S.A. (1982) *Managing Careers*. New York: Addison-Wesley.

McDonald, D.L. (2002) 'Career counseling strategies to facilitate the welfare-to-work transition: the case of Jeanetta', *Career Development Quarterly*, June.

McMahon, M. (2003) 'Supervision and career counsellors: a little explored practice with an uncertain future', *British Journal of Guidance and Counselling*, 31(2): 177–85.

Moreland, J.R. (1979) 'Some implications of life-span development for counseling psychology', *Personnel and Guidance Journal*, 57: 299–304.

Mulligan, J. (1988) *The Personal Management Handbook*. London: Sphere.

Nathan, R. (2003) 'Coaching with open ears', *People Management*, May 2003: 44.

Nathan, R. and Floyed, J. (2002) *The CCS Self-Assessment Manual*. London: Career Counselling Services.

Nelson-Jones, R. (1991) *Lifeskills: A Handbook*. London: Cassell Educational.

Newland Park Associates (1991) *Review of Psychometric Tests for Assessment in Vocational Training*. Leicester: British Psychological Society.

NICEC (2001) *The Impact of Careers Guidance Services for Employed People*. Cambridge: NICEC.

NICEC (2004) *Managing Careers in Large Organisations*. Cambridge: NICEC.

Oakeshott, M. (1991) *Educational Guidance for Adults: Identifying Competencies*. London: Further Education Unit, Leicester (Unit for the Development of Adult Continuing Education).

O'Connell, B. (1998) *Solution Focussed Therapy*. London: Sage.

Parsons, F. (1909) *Choosing a Vocation*. Boston, MA: Houghton-Mifflin.

Proctor, B. (1988) *Supervision: A Working Alliance* (Videotape Training Manual). St Leonards on Sea: Alexia.

Rogers, C. (1965) *On Becoming a Person*. London: Constable.

Schein, E.H. (1978) *Career Dynamics: Matching Individual and Organisational Needs*. New York: Addison-Wesley.

Schuller, T. and Walker, A. (1990) *The Time of Our Life: Education, Employment and Retirement in the Third Age*. London: Institute for Public Policy Research/Employment Paper 2.

Sheehy, G. (1976) *Passages: Predictable Crises of Adult Life*. London: Bantam.

Smith, M. (1989) *The Best Is Yet to Come: A Workbook for the Middle Years*. Sheffield: Lifeskills Associates.

Super, D.E. (1957) *The Psychology of Careers*. New York: Harper.

Super, D.E. (1980) 'A life-span, life-space approach to career development', *Journal of Vocational Behaviour*, 16: 282–98.

Taylor, N.B. (1985) 'How do career counsellors counsel?', *British Journal of Guidance and Counselling*, 13(2): 166–77.

Thomas, R.M. (1990) *Counseling and Life-Span Development*. Newbury Park, CA: Sage.

Whitmore, D. (1990) *Psychosynthesis Counselling in Action*. London: Sage.

Work-Family Research Newsletter www.bc.edu/bc_org/avp/wfnetwork/newsletter

Yost, E.B. and Corbishley, M.A. (1987) *Career Counselling: A Psychological Approach*. New York: Jossey-Bass.

Index